Footsteps to the Jungle

To my son 'Richard'

Footsteps to the Jungle

A Personal Journey

Penelope Worsley

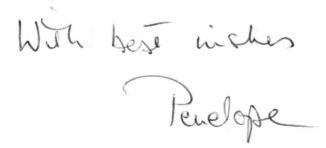

With best wishes

Penelope

Wharncliffe Books

First published in Great Britain in 2010 by
Wharncliffe Books
an imprint of
Pen and Sword Books Ltd
47 Church Street
Barnsley
South Yorkshire
S70 2AS

ISBN 978-1-84884-460-5

A CIP catalogue record for this book is available from the British Library.

Typeset in 11pt Ehrhardt by
Mac Style, Beverley, E. Yorkshire

Printed and bound in the UK by
CPI Antony Rowe, Chippenham, Wiltshire

Pen & Sword Books Ltd incorporates the imprints of Pen & Sword
Aviation, Pen & Sword Maritime, Pen & Sword Military, Wharncliffe
Local History, Pen & Sword Select, Pen & Sword Military Classics,
Leo Cooper, Seaforth Publishing and Frontline Publishing.

For a complete list of Pen & Sword titles please contact
PEN & SWORD BOOKS LIMITED
47 Church Street, Barnsley, South Yorkshire, S70 2AS, England
E-mail: enquiries@pen-and-sword.co.uk
Website: www.pen-and-sword.co.uk

Contents

List of Illustrations

Penelope aged two with her father on his return from the desert
Oliver and Penelope on their wedding day in 1966
Georgina, David, Penelope with Anne, Richard, Oliver
Mae Hong Son province and (inset) map of Thailand
The Richard Worsley Memorial Project 1997
Looking towards the Burma border
Salahae and his parents
Salahae with his wife Bo and children Fi and Jokasee
Richard and Salahae setting up a standpipe for the clean water tap
Penelope and Salahae at the clean water tap
Karen family in Ban Mae Yuam Luang
Family sorting sweet garlic
A local friend
Returning from fishing in the river
Old Karen lady
Man cutting bamboo
Oliver visiting the Karen in 2004
Karen granny with child
Clean water and no more typhoid
Fetching the logs for the fire
Richard visiting a village in 1990
Remote Karen house in 2009
Rice fields in June
Rice planting
Penelope sorting the rice
Pounding the rice
Weaving on a strap loom
Group of Karen women and children
Irrigation project. Water is channelled from river to the fields in canals
Newly regenerated land
Constructing water tanks
Volunteers celebrating the completion of a water system

List of Illustrations

Acknowledgements

Jim Soutar, without whom Richard would never have gone to Thailand.

My family who have put up with me during the difficult times and supported me in everything I have done. Above all, Oliver, who has been a wonderful husband and father; so patient and loving in spite of all his troubles.

Why I Wrote this Book

Even before Richard died I was struggling to cope. Every family has their difficulties, but somehow the speed with which things happened to me and the unusual events made it very difficult for me to share with others in a way that they could give me the support I needed. It seemed beyond comprehension. My daughter's story was so complex, so unbelievable and difficult for me, that over the years I had to write it down.

My son's death brought other issues and experiences which needed remembering and as time has gone by I have found that to share these experiences has helped me and comforted others in their grief. The work in Thailand, my knowledge of a large part of the northern region and the personal stories and lives of the Karen people that came as a result of Richard's death, has developed alongside all the family issues and in spite of them. For many years people have wondered where I get my energy from and how I have coped. My early childhood gave me skills which have been invaluable. Certainly Richard's death gave me a purpose in Thailand and a journey which seemed inevitable.

Although this book might seem like two different stories, all of it is integrated in my life in a way that makes them inseparable. I hope the experiences of Huntington's disease are helpful to others. The loss of a son, I feel, is good to share with others. The privilege of learning so much about a culture on the other side of the world has brought a richness that I treasure.

Eventually the charity will stand alone and hopefully continue to raise money and attract legacies so that it will continue to support the Karen people long after I have gone.

Although a great deal of research is being done on Huntington's disease, I cannot see any real change in the foreseeable future for those who have it except perhaps a better understanding of how to manage it and this comes from talking about it; but for me they remain real issues with which I need to deal with, and I will.

I hope that you find encouragement and some amusement in some small way in this book.

Preface

Wat Prabhat Huay Tom – and the Footprints of Khru Ba

The name is explained like this: Wat means 'temple'. Prabhat means 'footprint of Buddha', and Huay means 'small river' or 'stream'. Tom means 'boil'.

Wat Prabhat Huay Tom is situated 150 kilometres south of Chiang Mai in the district of Lamphun in northwest Thailand. Taking the road due south of Hod on Route 108 you pass through the small town of Li and find the main entrance to the village on your right. The straight road ahead of you takes you past small, poor Karen stilted houses and more roads at right angles to other parts of the village. At the end of the first road is a large white temple, obviously still under construction. I came here a few years ago when Salahae, now our Karen manager, brought me to see how the silver jewellery was made. I knew that this was the only village in the whole of Thailand where the Karen silver is made, but I had no idea why and I had no idea about the history of this village. It was, even then, the largest number of Karen people living in one village and today has a population of 15,000 people.

All around is flat country with no mountains in sight. It is largely uninteresting; there are no rice fields and no obvious reason why the Karen people would live here. I had first come to see the silver because we wanted to sell it in the UK not just to raise extra funds but also to raise the profile of the skills of the Karen people.

It was here on my second visit in 2009 that I learnt more about this village and the history of Khru Ba Chaiwongsa. He was the visionary monk who died in 2001 and whose body is embalmed in gold leaf and set very high in a huge glass case in one of the most amazingly spectacular temples I have seen. Charmingly, in spite of all the gold leaf, he is still wearing his woolly hat! I have written more about this village and the history of the Karen people and the leadership of this remarkable and talented visionary monk later in the book, but it was here that I saw two huge footprint shaped spaces set onto a large square marble topped plinth that depicted the footsteps of Khru Ba. It was like a tomb itself and obviously revered. A long length of bamboo was arranged so that on occasions water can be channelled into the footprint spaces. The actual stone marked with the real footprints is preserved under the footprint baths that we could see. The story of the footprints are also illustrated amongst the many paintings surrounding this huge temple.

This image so gripped me that when I was pulling together the contents of this book, it gave me the title and Anno Domini permitting, I still hope to make a few more footsteps.

Penelope Worsley
June 2010

PART I

Chapter One

Richard's Death

I was sound asleep. I don't go to bed very early, but when I do, I sleep very soundly. Oliver was away. He had been staying with his brother in Canada and would be arriving home on that Monday. Deep in my slumber I could hear this bell ringing. I woke and turned on the light. The doorbell was still ringing. It was 4.00am. I did not think very much. I just crawled out of bed to find out who it was. For some reason I was not worried about whom it may be. I was too sleepy for that. In a dressing gown, with no slippers I opened the door to find an army officer standing there. He said: "I am sorry to wake you, Ma'am, but I have some bad news for you. Your son Richard has been involved in a bad car accident in Germany. I am afraid he is dead."

I can remember thinking: "This is what happens to other people and now it is my turn!" I was trying hard to focus and keep calm. I asked the officer if he would like to come in and have a cup of coffee, but he would not. He asked if I was okay. I said I was and thanked him for telling me. I can remember thinking how awful for him to have to tell me this news. He had been the duty officer at Leconfield that night and had been sent to tell me quickly in case the press told me first. I appreciated that. The next few hours before the day was to dawn gave me time to think; time to plan. Somehow I just accepted that Richard had died. I did not question it. Somehow I suppose, I had been expecting it; or was it that I was never surprised by what happened next in life?

Richard had died at 12.20am on the infamous tank road between Hohne and Fallingbostel in northern Germany. He was travelling as a passenger with a fellow regimental officer to another regiment where he would be better briefed before going to his new posting on attachment in Northern Ireland. The inquest said that they were probably travelling at around seventy to seventy-five miles an hour. There was a bend in the road and something happened and their car turned over in the forest and they were both killed instantly; no one witnessed it so no one really knew the finer details. Richard had been looking forward to his time in Northern Ireland. He knew it would be tough but it would be a challenge. He had joined the Light Dragoons when he was twenty-one and was now to be attached to the Royal Tank Regiment for six months' tour in Northern Ireland. He had already been to Bosnia. He had been the first person to drive his armoured reconnaissance vehicle into Ban Yaluka. It had been filmed for BBC News. There he was on the national news on News Year's Day in January 1996, leading his troop into Ban Yaluka. We were so proud. He looked so young. He still seemed to have his "bum fluff". He hardly shaved at all. The last time we had seen Richard was at his cousin Giles' wedding several months ago. All dressed up in his morning suit, he had looked a little thin on top, but then his father started to go bald at that age.

Now he was dead at twenty-four years old. My thoughts took me back. The last time Richard was home, we had taken him to the Mystery Plays in York Theatre Royal. Richard sat in the row behind us and immediately introduced himself to the people sitting next to him and explained he had just come back from Bosnia. They had been delighted with this friendship. The very same people that he sat next to were to tell me this ten years later when I was giving a talk about the charity. The day after the trip to the theatre he had heard news that his good friend Richard (Dicky) Madden of the Light Dragoons had been blown up in his Spartan armoured vehicle in Bosnia. Richard was devastated and he quickly rang Dicky's mother and was later privileged to carry his coffin. These moments found Richard and I talking about death. What would happen if Richard died? How would Richard feel about this? What would he want us to do, if he died? He was very philosophical: of course it would be a tragedy and something he would rather not happen, but if it did we were to think positively about the good things. Now he was dead. I had to be positive.

Years ago, my own mother had said to me: "Don't love your children too much, because they will be taken from you. Something will happen." I remembered these words now.

I started to make lists. My husband Oliver was on his way back from staying with his brother in Canada and was not expected home until later in the day. My children, Georgina, David and Anne would have to be told as early as possible that morning.

Georgina my eldest daughter was twenty-eight. She had been living in France with her two children, Molly and Marcus. She had arrived in London on the Sunday and rang me to ask for help. She had no money and nowhere to live. This was the latest chapter in years of problems and I had told her that she would have to sort out her problems and could not come home. Now twenty-four hours later, I had to tell her that Richard was dead and she would have to come home. She caught the same train as David and Anne from London, moved into Richard's bedroom and stayed for six months.

Richard's Death

Anne was twenty-two when Richard died. She had been with him in Germany for a weekend of fun and regimental parties and returned to London only a few hours before he was killed. She adored Richard. He was such fun, slightly crazy at times, but always interested in others, always in touch. Richard in turn was very proud of Anne, now a trained nurse she was on duty at the National Hospital for Neurology and Neurosurgery in Queen's Square in London. I had to ring the Sister on the ward and tell her what had happened and ask her to send someone to be with Anne when I told her the news. There was a silence, a sense of real shock, but she knew that she had to come home with David and Georgina.

I began to telephone other members of the family and the news began to spread. Inside me there grew a burning passion that I had to tell people, that I had to tell people all about Richard. There was something a bit different about Richard. I had to make sure that he was not forgotten, that his character would be remembered. His great enthusiasm for life, for people – he had always loved people. I had not felt this great urgency about Richard since he was born. He was born on October 11th in 1974. He was my third child and I thought I knew what childbirth felt like; but as Richard arrived in the world something extraordinary happened to my emotions. They went sky high. I felt I had to tell the highest people in the church that this baby was something special in the world. I felt he should have a very special blessing.

I didn't tell anyone about this feeling as my days with the new baby were busy and maybe I was a little overwhelmed and unrealistic, but certainly something extraordinary hit me emotionally when he was born. Now I got this feeling again. I had to make sure that as many people as possible knew that he had died.

I searched through his contacts and in the process remembered that when he was nineteen and before Sandhurst, he had gone to Thailand to work with the Karen hill tribes to install clean water systems. He had gone to work with someone called Jim who was encouraging young people to help in this way. Richard had had a privileged background; a good home, a good education at Bramcote Preparatory School in Scarborough and then Uppingham School in Leicestershire. Now he felt the need to go and live with people of another culture who have nothing, before he went on to join the army. He wanted to experience what it was like to live in the forests in a bamboo house, to work in the rice fields, to carve your own tools and make rafts to get across the river. He ate snakes, rats and lots of rice. Richard had had a wonderful time. He came home bubbling with enthusiasm. "Mummy I have had the most amazing time, but I do hope you will help these people one day," he said, "because they really need your help."

Now I had to tell Jim that Richard was dead. I faxed him quickly. Within forty-eight hours came back four pages of emotion telling me how much they had enjoyed this rather brash English public school boy. They had never met anyone quite like Richard before. He wrote: "Karen folklore says that 'Good men do not die. They stay as stars in the sky to guide us, for ever." I printed an extract of his response in a book I wrote for Richard's funeral.

The following words were written by Jim Soutar, the Director of the Ruamkanpattana Foundation in Thailand, as soon as he heard of Richard's death.

If I could sum up Richard's year among the hilltribes of northwest Thailand, I would have to be as totally frank as Richard himself always was. He came to us straight from his final year at public school. He was the archetypal upper-class English public schoolboy: brash, self-confident, experienced in the reality of human dynamics; self-assured, vulnerable, loving, caring, decent. He was ever most frighteningly and effervescently ebullient, to the extent that we, in the Foundation, were continually in a situation of wondering what he would do next. But he never did wrong. He had this innate 'correctness', this desire to help those less fortunate than himself, an ability to transpose his own family background and his school experience into a self-defined and self created methodology, fine-tuned to assist the hilltribes of the mountain forests into which he had chosen to be transported. He was magnificently, and at times infuriatingly, irrepressible. He accepted any challenge, even to the point of bravado, but always with his own so definable panache.

What we in the Foundation particularly liked about our good friend Richard was his totally dedicated commitment to whatever he was doing at the time. If we were digging trenches through steep forest slopes to take water pipes to a remote and impoverished village, Richard was forever there at the front of the line of villagers, laughing, joking, drinking the local 'moonshine whisky' – in brief, being totally at one with the hilltribe villagers and their virtually primordial existence; and always, always showing, sometimes ostentatiously, but most often more discreetly, his own and already very much defined personal code of leadership. In administrative matters he could be absolutely frustrating. He would say to us, "Let's do it, and someone else can write about it afterwards!" But who had the unenviable task of writing it up afterwards? Richard himself. His reports were succinct, indeed terse, but they were always totally accurate.

The Karen had never met anyone like Richard Worsley; neither had we, in the more sophisticated environs of Bangkok. He was, above all, his own man. He loved life, and he transmitted his great love of life to all those with whom he interfaced. He was eccentric, sometimes infuriating, but he was loved more deeply by the Karen than many, many other foreigners that they had met and lived with. He had a way with people, a way that made them feel that he was a natural leader – if only he would accept the challenge and burden of leadership.

We loved Richard. At times, if he wanted to be, he could be maddeningly frustrating; but he was always of such a deeply sincere honesty and decency, coupled with his incredibly refreshing and constant sense of humour, that it was natural for all of us in the Foundation to just love him. And now Richard has gone before us that will not change. His zest for life, his deep-felt humanitarianism, and his acute personal dynamism are here with us now, and will remain with us, as long as those of us who remember Richard Worsley are still alive under the panoply of the stars. The Karen hilltribes, in their cultural folklore, believe that true friends and true leaders, the two being so often synonymous to the Karen, will become stars in the heavens when they die. We, the staff of the Ruamkanpattana Foundation, will examine the stars in the coming winter sky. In the mountains of northern Thailand, the night sky is vast. We will find our friend Richard there, and we will be glad that our friend is there to guide us. The Karen believes that a good man does not die. His goodness remains with and in all of us, and he checks from the sky that we are following his example.

Richard Worsley gave us that example. We deeply mourn his passing from among us, but his example remains to guide us.

From the starry sky, Richard, may you achieve those goals of love and honour that your short life denied you to achieve on this sublunary abode.

Extract from a letter dated 27 November 1996.

I gathered other material for his funeral book including:

An abiding memory from Uppingham

Richard had five years of constant, personal development and achievement in the school. He was successfully involved, among many other things, as an able and creative A level designer, an enthusiastic and committed CCF cadet officer and an excellent and generous House Captain. The most important and enduring memory for those who shared with him a part or all those five years, was of a contemporary who was never unkind in word or deed to others and never in thought either, one suspected. This was a very special and wonderful quality to find in a young man and was especially so for those who lived alongside him.

Martin Bell (the BBC correspondent) wrote:

> The Light Dragoons became almost the adopted Regiment of the BBC team
> working in Bosnia – and Richard was certainly one of its brightest lights. His
> Squadron Commander used to speak of the Cavalry's 'charm and guile'. I
> don't know about the guile, but he certainly had the charm – plus courage
> and good humour and unwavering kindness to others. When beset by war
> zone despair I would remember him and take heart. I still do. The very best
> example of a man.

We knew it would be a big funeral. We had to put a large marquee extension
on the back of the beautiful Saxon church at Hovingham so that everyone
could see and hear. We wanted everyone to feel part of the funeral, so the
service was relayed onto large screens in the extension. His troop carried
his coffin in full military dress with all the discipline that is so moving to
watch. Richard had adored the army. The camaraderie, the challenges and
the discipline. He loved polishing his boots and marching up and down.
Even if he came home on leave he would be practising his marching, up
and down, and always made sure his shoes were shining bright! His troop
loved him in so far as soldiers can. He had always made sure that his troop
was cared for. They were 'his' men and they really mattered to him. He
knew that without his men he could not be a true officer and fight the
battles that he might be asked to fight. They had shared the same tank in
Bosnia and now they were carrying his coffin. I went across to talk to them
and thank them for all they had done for him.

The music was wonderful. The family read poems and his fellow officers
talked of their memories. At least six hundred people came to the service
and half of those followed the coffin to the cemetery where he was buried
with full military honours. It was a proud and sad moment as we were
handed his cap, his medal and the regimental flag, which had been laid on
his coffin.

So to finish the day we had a party in the Riding School at Hovingham
Hall for all those who had come so far to bid him farewell. We had
champagne. Richard had adored champagne; just like his father he could
drink champagne any hour of the day. When he was eighteen he had gone
to work with Mercier in France as a stagier. To have champagne at his
funeral was just what he would have liked.

After Richard's funeral there was a lot to do. There were hundreds of
letters to answer and Richard's possessions to sort out. He did not possess
much, but the little he had, had to go somewhere. How, where and why do

you keep the possessions of those who have died? Do you put them in a box, or do you give them away? Apart from his clothes, and much of those were regimental, there was not much else. There were his school reports and design projects from his A levels. There were all those regimental photographs.

Then there was the bowler hat. This wretched bowler hat had caused me such a lot of hassle! Richard had been asked to steward at the Great Yorkshire Show for several years, but all stewards had to wear a bowler hat to distinguish them to the public. The trouble was that Richard had such a large head and no one could lend him one. As it was only needed for four days a year there seemed no point in spending a lot of money on a new one but eventually there was no way out of it. We just had to help him buy one and it cost a lot of money. He just wore it for the one season of four days and now what was I to do with it?

He collected old cameras and catalogued his photographs meticulously but there was nothing special there. Then there was the little leather suitcase. He had taken it all over the world. It was so battered and the stitching was going, but it was good leather and it had a history to tell. Richard loved the good things in life and this good leather case was something special to him. I still have this but it would cost too much to mend, so it just sits in a cupboard. There was something very final about getting rid of his things, so we had to keep a bit.

Some people said they could not bear to have a photograph on show after they had lost their son. In the end, we put his photograph and a book of remembrance, his regimental cap and medals on display in the hall where they are seen all the year round by all our visitors and where we can pause from time to time in the busy day. The large regimental flag that covered his coffin hangs on the wall on the stairs.

I kept a small box of things that were totally random and utterly useless, but I kept them all the same. They included letters from girl friends and notes to friends. He had some lovely girl friends and they were so devastated by his death. That was all there was left, or so I thought.

Chapter Two

The Dreams and the Spirits

Richard had died on November 25th in 1996 and he was buried at Hovingham on 4th December. On Christmas Day Oliver and I went to Sung Eucharist in York Minster, it was all very difficult and sad. Richard was not with us, and then Oliver had this strange feeling that Richard was talking to him. He tried to say that they had not been driving too fast when they had the car accident. Oliver remembered it very clearly. He also seemed to be telling Oliver that he, Richard, would look after him. At the time I tossed it out of my mind, as being something that Oliver wanted to believe.

Then Anne had a dream; she rang me to say she had had this terrible dream. She had been sitting on a bench and the coffin was being carried past her with Richard's body, but the coffin was in flames. She was devastated by this dream. When Richard's body had been brought back to England it was badly damaged. Undertakers try hard to rebuild bodies so that the family can see their loved ones in the Chapel of Rest. David and Georgina had chosen to see him, but Anne did not want to. At the funeral she could not touch the coffin because of the formalities. She felt somehow cheated of this goodbye. Whether the dream had any connection with these thoughts no one will ever know. It was all too close for comfort. She had sobbed and sobbed.

Soon after, maybe February of the following year, Oliver had another dream. He was driving a car with Richard in the passenger seat. They were driving through an army camp and as Oliver dropped Richard off at the gates he said: "You will be alright now," and then he disappeared. Eight years later and the dreams were still very vivid to Oliver.

A year after Richard died I was talking to a friend about these dreams and she asked me if I had had my dream yet. I asked her why I should have a dream? "Well you will," she said. It was another year before I had a dream. There he was. I had walked into this dark room. It was black except for the rectangular plain wooden table in the middle of the room. Sitting at the far end was Richard, dressed in his dark green jersey with his cavalry twill trousers. He had crossed his arms. As I came into the room, he got up and slowly came toward me. He put his arms around me and gave me a big gentle hug. I remember saying and thinking that I knew he was dead. "I know you are dead. I know you are dead." I said it several times as if to reassure myself that it could not be really him, but I knew it was. As he hugged me he gently disappeared and I woke up.

A few years later I was looking in the photograph album and there was Richard in the very jersey that I saw him wearing in my dream. I could not help feeling that maybe his spirit was still around.

David had two experiences. Eight years after Richard died, he talked to me about them. He was not sure how to describe the first one. It might have been a vision or a sensation? He described it like this:

"The night that I returned to London after the funeral, I had tucked myself up in bed and was ready to fall asleep. I had just turned the light out. My bed was in a corner away from the door and I could feel this 'energy' in the far corner of the room. It came towards me, very positively, and then the 'energy' seemed to have movement. It got half way across the room and as it came I turned over towards the wall, pulling the bedclothes over my head. I pulled my knees up to my chest. I was absolutely terrified. I huddled under the covers, shaking in fear. After a short time, the energy disappeared and the room was calm again. At the time I did not connect it with Richard and it is only years later that I really connect it with him. I feel now that he was trying to reach me, and I turned my back and rejected him.

The second time it was a dream, but I only remember the end of it. There was a road and the weather was hot. There were quite a lot of people. There was a car. I was just looking about and I suddenly spotted Richard and I was very surprised to see him. I was really elated. It was so exciting! I ran towards him and leapt into his arms and hugged him. At the time it just felt so right to be with Richard again. It was as if I had lost him and now I had found him and it was a wonderful feeling, then I woke up."

David goes on: "Even now, I find it very difficult to cope with Richard's death, because he is not here and it was only a dream. I still cannot touch him and perhaps the dreams show me how much I really want him back. After he died I kept wanting to touch him and it was (and still is) terrible not to be able to feel his body."

Later, when he was at the Royal College of Art, David made an exhibition piece around Richard's death. He lay in a coffin every day of the exhibition (with the lid down) to try and experience what it must have been like for Richard.

In the months following Richard's death, I often wondered about him. People told me that he was still around and that I would dream and that he would speak to me, but I was puzzled and curious. Out of sheer curiosity, only a few months after Richard died, I made an appointment to see a clairvoyant/medium in York. He told me things that did not mean much and I was disappointed that he had not picked up that Richard had died. I told him that Richard had died a few months before and I wanted to know whether he could send any messages. I was told that when someone dies so suddenly it takes time for the 'spirit' to settle. It would be at least a year before Richard would communicate. I was very disappointed. I don't know why, because I did not expect to believe anything that I was told, I thought although it would have been comforting. I did not tell anyone that I had made this visit because I knew they would be cynical.

Georgina had always had an interest in "alternative" medicine; "alternative" ways of looking at things. Clairvoyants, mediums, swinging pendulums, were all helpful in confirming to her that her destiny was written in front of her. About a year after Richard died, she discovered the Spiritualist Association in London and called in, without an appointment. Sitting with a group of people she had never met before she was singled out. Thinking that she would be told about where she might live next or some exciting adventure that might befall her, she was surprised to be told: "There is a young man with military connections who is trying to tell you …"

So Anne decided to call there too. Again, without giving any recognition of who she was or why she was there, she was told that there was a young man with military connections who is trying to tell her something, but again nothing further.

I could not resist it. I too made an appointment. In the first minute the man told me that there was a young man with military connections who wanted to tell me that he was so sad he had not gone to Northern Ireland (Ireland had been his next posting). He was okay in his new world. He spent time marching up and down polishing his army boots. He wanted to say that at the time of the car accident they had not been driving too fast. He was very sad about it all. The medium asked if there was anything else I would like to know. I asked if there was any sign of my mother or father (they had died over twenty years previously). He said there was a man who was busy gardening. He was wearing a brown tweed jacket. Did this mean anything to me? My father had one of the finest gardens in the west of England and was passionate about it. He always wore a brown tweed jacket. "And what about my mother," I asked. I was told, "There is a woman who has not come over the bridge to talk to you, but she is surrounded by young people and seems quite happy. She seems to have a large black dog with her." My mother bred black Labradors and always enjoyed the company of young people.

I began to feel that there really was another world up there and I began to feel rather excited. It sounded as if one day I would see Richard again. Who knows? I got the feeling that Richard really was in touch with us and watching over us.

It was not for another two years that I went again and discovered more.

Chapter Three

Richard and His Time in Thailand

Richard had grown up in the East Riding of Yorkshire where we farmed. He helped with the lambs and earned his pocket money driving the garden tractor. He loved being at home. He had been to the local primary school and had enjoyed camping and the involvement with charity work. He loved people, just as I do. He remembered people and they remembered him, he looked you straight in the eyes and took an interest. Some children are like that, but many are not. It was just the way he was. He was determined to join the British Army, but before he did that, he was determined to go and live with another culture. He knew he had had a privileged upbringing and it was very important to him to find out what life was like for those who have nothing. A friend had already been to Thailand and enjoyed it and after a little research we discovered Jim, who had eventually written the words that we printed in his funeral book.

At the time, Jim was based in Bangkok and had been working with the Karen people for a number of years. He knew their need for clean water but lacked the funds to buy the materials. For various reasons he linked with Gordonstoun school to help with funding and labour to install clean water systems. The result was that he encouraged a few other young people like Richard to come and experience life with the Karen people.

Richard was interviewed by Jim's friend Michael in Oxford and set off for Thailand in January 1990. During the next six months he travelled throughout Thailand, making the most of the beautiful beaches on Kho Samui and Kho Pak Nam and Kho Tai, learning to dive and enjoying the beautiful girls. He travelled to Ayutayah and up to Chiang Mai. He enjoyed Jim's company, as did so many others. They talked of life and drank the 'moonshine' (the local rice whisky). He made friends with Jim's family and developed a wonderful friendship with all those in the village of Mae Phon, north of Chom Thong. Mae Phon was a pretty village high in the mountains. There was a large dormitory there, run by the nuns of the Congregation of the Mission Etranger de Paris (MEP) from France. It was known as the Karen Hill Tribe Centre. Father Jo was in charge of the "community" and Richard made great friends with him. Sister Cecile also knew Richard. Now retired, when I went to see her in 2003 she remembered Richard well.

Helping Jim was a Karen called Chompon. I don't know a lot about Chompon, but I know from Richard and others who knew him that he was a good man and a family man. He was married with two children. Richard sent him a large parcel of toys when he returned to the UK. He and Richard had laughed and worked together and made good friends. Other volunteers used to come and stay with Jim and found friendship with Chompon too.

One of the difficulties that are often encountered is that English people don't take time to listen to the Karen people. They need to watch and listen and not assume they can do the same as they can in the UK. Years later I was told about Sarah, a young volunteer like Richard who was there about the same time. Sarah had asked him: "May I go with you to hunt? I know you have to climb the tree and I want to go." Chompon said "No." "Why?" said Sarah. Chompon said that it was totally unacceptable for a woman to go hunting. It is taboo. Sarah said this was just superstitious and she wanted to go. But Chompon was adamant. This fear had come from generations ago. The deer would come if the woman went hunting and there would be many problems. Sarah said: "I have just graduated from Oxford and we are very clever there. We understand what is safe and what is not." Chompon got very angry indeed. He said: "You are clever in Oxford but not here. You cannot understand." Sarah cried a lot, said my friend.

Chompon's main job was to work on the water systems and at that time he had help from a young man called Salahae. Salahae took Richard to stay with his own family for a whole week near the town of Khun Yuam. He made him the machete that I have today.

A letter from Richard reports how they snared a giant rat snake. Salahae's father fried it with garlic, ginger, turmeric and lemon grass. He wrote, "It was delicious!"

Salahae remembers Richard for his fun, laughter and hard work and his ability to get on with anyone. Salahae took Richard, Will Silverwood Cope and Chris Hardie who were working with him as volunteers, to the village of Ban Rak Mai Nua where they helped to install a water system. It was here that Richard spent three weeks, working hard alongside the Karen people, joining with them in the excitement of having clean water and knowing that their health would improve dramatically.

28

They had many adventures; Richard talked of his time and showed me photographs of the snakes and the bugs, but also of the children who had sung songs with him and helped to dig trenches.

Chris Hardie wrote of his memories:

"One incident in particular stands out. We were in a village (Ban Rak Mai Nua) doing a project and the villagers were demonstrating their tarantula catching skills. They were dug out of their nests in the ground and later cooked on the fire for a treat. Richard managed to get hold of one of the tarantulas (he was brave enough to pick it up) and crept up behind Will and put it on his back. When Will realized he had an enormous spider crawling over his shoulder he went bananas (I think ripping his shirt off in the process) and had a complete sense of humour failure. The rest of us found it very funny indeed.

Throughout his time in Thailand, I remember Richard being tremendously enthusiastic and often taking the lead in situations where we were happy to sit back a bit. During the evenings when we were asked to perform songs in front of the assembled village he would get us all going with numbers such as 'If you're happy and you know it'. He was always popular with the villagers and a source of great interest and amusement. I seem to remember at one point him putting it about that he was unusually 'well hung'. I'm not sure exactly how he did this, but it made the villagers, particularly the women all the more curious!

I had come out with a new camera that I had no idea how to use properly. I remember Richard having a real interest in photography and very patiently teaching me the basics.

I also remember his interest in enormous Rambo style knives; he was off to the army after all. He acquired a number of fearsome weapons in Thailand, getting progressively bigger and more dangerous looking and would take great delight in showing them off despite our groans! I'm not sure if he was able to bring any of these back to the UK, but I've no doubt that he tried."

Chapter Four

My Early Years and Life Experiences

It occurred to me that it was much of the experiences of my childhood and earlier life that gave me the strength and skills to cope with the life ahead of me. Life is a journey and I felt I was only halfway through.

I was born in Cairo in 1942. My parents were married on 12 September in 1939, just after the war broke out. Soon after that my father was posted to Egypt where he was a staff officer to Field Marshall Lord Montgomery. He was responsible for writing the dispatches that were sent back to King George VI for 'his eyes only'. He was based in Cairo, but much of his work was in the desert with the 8th Army. Women were not allowed to be in Cairo during the war but my mother, a woman of some determination, decided she would not be left behind. I remember her saying that no women were allowed to join their husbands in such places. However she had soon persuaded the relevant department in the UK to allow her to join the VAD (Voluntary Aid Detachment) in Cairo. Unable to tell him of her new job, she arrived in Cairo and sent him a message to say "his baggage had arrived and was awaiting collection at the Shepherd's Hotel." During the next five years my mother offered hospitality to those coming back from the desert who needed rest and recuperation and together they made many friends. Every time the government tried to send her back to the UK she was too pregnant to travel. I was the eldest, my sister Victoria was born fifteen months later and my brother Charles was 'on the way' when my parents returned to England. My younger sister Georgina was born nine years younger than me.

After the war, I grew up in Wiltshire at Corsham near Bath. My father had inherited a house, but the furniture was left to his sisters, so the house was empty. All their possessions they had in Cairo were bombed on the way home. There was not much money to buy anything. Food was rationed. We had powdered eggs, sweets were a rare treat and if I was lucky I had one packet of polo sweets to last me a whole week.

Shoes were always passed on to another member of the family. I remember the cupboard in the attic where the long shelves were filled with shoes waiting to be handed down. We did not wear socks in the summer, so our heels had to be rubbed with spirit to harden the skin and prevent us getting blisters.

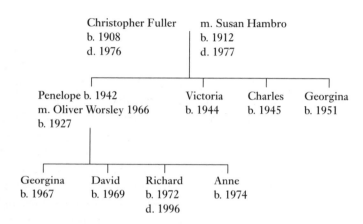

My father worked in London when he was a director of the family brewery Fuller Smith & Turner and my mother spent a greater part of the week in London to support him. We were brought up by a nanny and had a governess till I was eleven years old. We had lessons with the children from the naval camp over the fields. My childhood was fun. We picnicked in hay fields, collected and pressed wild flowers, spent holidays at the seaside, and we saw our parents at weekends and in the evenings, if they were home.

Then I went to St Mary's School in Wantage, a convent boarding school. It had a junior school at Pangbourne right out in the country. There were lots of woods and we played for hours making dens amongst the trees. Always bottom of the class; my birthday was in August so I was always the youngest at least that was my excuse. I left school just before my sixteenth birthday with only two GCSE's under my belt; English Language and Art. "There was no point in her staying any longer," said Sister Honor Margaret, "as I don't think she could complete her A levels."

So I went to London for three months and learnt 'public speaking', took up a secretarial course and learnt some French before spending six months in Paris at the Sorbonne University. Then there was a season in London. There were lots of parties; coffee parties, lunch parties, cocktail parties, dinner parties, weekend parties. The idea was to meet lots of people and it was very necessary to learn how to network. If not, you may not get a lift home or find a husband. I had a job at the same time, working in advertising and television, but soon I had a secretary of my own and was building a small business in an estate agency, letting sporting rights in Scotland, Yorkshire and Iceland.

Throughout my life I had always been involved with fundraising. As a child, I followed my mother to the village hall and helped with the teas and the bric a brac stalls. When I grew up I joined the St John Ambulance as a cadet in Wiltshire. This continued after I went to live in London, and every week I was out on a Thursday night, training or on duty, in uniform, serving the public with the St John Ambulance. I absolutely loved it. I was desperate to go to Cyprus in 1958 and was so disappointed when they told me I was not old enough and did not have enough experience.

I had always wanted to go to Australia and travel but I never had enough cash for anything much. I lived with my parents in London, but I could not really afford the rent, let alone go travelling. Then one day I was returning to London by train on a Sunday evening from my home in Wiltshire. On the same train was an elderly Australian couple called Margaret and George, who had been visiting some cousins of mine. Margaret was sixty years old, I was nineteen, and they seemed to me quite elderly. We got chatting and I voiced my interest in visiting Australia. Before we got to London, they had asked me if I would like to join them on a flight in a six-seater Piper Aztec aeroplane that they were taking on a delivery flight to Sydney. It would take a month to get there. There was one big problem and that was that they were leaving on Thursday and I would need eight visas. I did not even have a passport. The one I had was Egyptian and I was under twenty-one years old and therefore not responsible enough to sign documents. My father was in the north of Scotland stalking deer in the mountains and could not be reached; without his signature, there would be no passport. No passport, no visas.

Mum went into overdrive. She had not flinched when told of this mad idea, that her eldest daughter was going to set off on this amazing flight, not knowing where she would end up or when she would be back. She gave me huge encouragement and the first thing she did was to find the head man at Passport House. Turning on all the charm, she told him of this forthcoming potential trip and begged him to find a way of getting round the 'passport issue'. He agreed to allow my father to telegraph his signature to Passport

House and the passport would be fast tracked. In the meantime Mum dragged me round the eight embassies, telling them of the story and begging them to fast track the visas, and she succeeded. By the time we got the passport, all the embassies were ready with the relevant documents. Unfortunately there was a train strike on the Wednesday and I needed to get some summer clothes from my home in Wiltshire, so that delayed everything. The shops did not sell summer clothes in October in 1959. I left a day late and joined Margaret and George in Rome.

From there we dropped down every six hundred miles en route to Australia. The plane was not pressurized; there were no toilets on board, no way to stand up, no room for extra luggage. Our route took us to Paris, Rome, Athens, Beirut (stayed a week), Sharjah, Karachi, Delhi, Calcutta, Rangoon, Bangkok (three days), Singapore, Djakarta, Bali, Portuguese Timor and Darwin. Then on to 'station country' in Queensland and out into the bush to boil the billy can before flying on to Sydney Smith airport in New South Wales. It had taken us twenty-eight days to fly from the UK to Sydney in Australia.

Here we got a very special welcome as our pilot, Sammy Dodd, had flown this little plane solo across the Azores from America to bring it to the UK on a delivery flight to a station in New South Wales, Australia. It had been quite scary at times, although more so for Margaret as she understood the consequences, particularly flying down the gulf over Syria. There were huge sandstorms and not being pressurized we could not fly above 10,000 ft. If we flew below 4,000 ft we ran the risk that we would be shot down. So it was a very bumpy ride to Sharjah!

My journey to Australia was something special that I was not going to forget and on this journey, it was Bangkok that seemed to be the highlight. We spent three days there. We had to travel as 'staff' to make the airport admin easier. I was the Purser while the others were Air Hostess and Co Pilot. So as we landed in Bangkok I had to deal with the landing fees, £90 for three days. We were horrified, but we had a lot of fun. It was October, it was the King's birthday and every few years, he celebrates by taking the Royal Barges down the river. In 1960, this is exactly what happened. These amazingly beautiful carved wooden barges paraded down the river. We made trips to the Floating Market and saw Bangkok as it was then.

From Sydney I hitched a lift and caught a bus and travelled to Melbourne, across to Adelaide and then spent five months in Perth where I stayed with my godfather who was the Governor of Western Australia, General Sir Charles Gairdner. I returned on the liner Canberra on which I had found myself a job as a PA to Sir Charles as he left Perth for the last time as Governor. I had worked as a photographic model in Perth, and earned money as a TV hostess on a quiz programme. I had left England at four days' notice and was away ten months and it had only cost me £250. I was very, very lucky and had an amazing time. I was always grateful for my mother's encouragement, trust and support.

I suppose this is what drives me on to encourage young people today to do exciting things, slightly out of one's comfort zone, always stretching and challenging. It gives me a great thrill to find the young people wanting to get out there, in the big wide world.

It was strange coming back to London after a year away and such an adventure. However I settled back into office life in London for another four years. I was still meeting new people and developed friends all over England. One such friend was David Gundry. He lived with his mother in Hovingham, a small village in north Yorkshire. I had been asked by David to join him on a yacht sailing round Corfu which I absolutely loved. Then I was invited to his twenty-first birthday party which was held in Hovingham Hall, the home of the Worsley family who had lived there for 400 years. It was a big party and we stayed in house parties nearby for the whole weekend. It was at this party that I met my future husband, Oliver. (David Gundry was killed at the age of twenty-four, in a road accident just outside York and is buried a few yards from where Richard is now buried.)

Oliver was the second son of Sir William and Lady Worsley. He had two brothers and a sister. He was living at Givendale, near Pocklington in the East Riding of Yorkshire where he farmed. He was very well known in the area and everybody loved him. He was hunting and point-to-pointing and I was often there at weekends to cheer him on in the races or take him to hospital when he had an accident following a fall off his horse, which happened fairly frequently. It was all fun. After I had known him about three months, he asked me to marry him. I was so surprised, I said, "I cannot possibly marry you, I have only known you three months. Why don't we think about it for six months and see how we feel then?" Six months went by and he said no more. Oh dear, I thought. He is not going to mention it; and actually I think it would be a really good idea. So I took courage in both hands and said to him: "You know you asked me to marry you a few months ago, well I think it would be wonderful." "Oh dear," said Oliver. I am not at all certain now." Another six months went by and he tried again, but I felt all this to and fro-ing was not good and I really was not sure. Four years later, in July 1966, I was staying with him again for the York Festival of which he was chairman. We had been to a recital of the Monteverdi Vespers in York Minster and were due to go out to lunch with friends afterwards. Oliver changed the plans and instead we set off for lunch with his parents. On the way, along the top road from Givendale to Birdsall, just as the road drops off the edge of the Wolds and overlooking the vast expanse of the Vale of York, he stopped the car and told me we were going to lunch at Hovingham and he wanted to tell them that we would get married. So he asked me what I would say? I was so taken aback that I said: "I suppose so."

So, at the age of twenty-four I married Oliver, who was then thirty-nine. We were married in my home town of Corsham in Wiltshire. A train load of friends and regimental colleagues from the Yeomanry came down for the day, 700 people came and it was a beautiful wedding. We honeymooned in the West Indies and I went to live in Yorkshire to share Oliver's life. I spent time with my charity work, running events, chairing various committees and endlessly raising money. Oliver was busy hunting and point-to-pointing. It was a bit smart for me, so I did a lot of the grooming and 'mucking out' the stable and looking after him when he fell off, which seemed often. We had Shetland ponies and dogs, as well as sheep around the house. I used to help with the lambing, taking my turn on the night shift. Apart from running a large country house and entertaining those who came to stay, we had two children; Georgina was born in 1967 and David was born in 1969.

In addition we also ran a restaurant; a French one in a beautiful building on the main street into York, known as Micklegate. We had a lot of fun although neither of us knew anything about the business. I used to clean out the loos in the morning and arrange the flowers while Oliver organized the wine. We ran special profile events to bring in the customers. That lasted three years until the chef gave notice when I was eight months pregnant with Richard. I decided enough was enough and we sold it. I continued with St John Ambulance, setting up cadet and adult divisions (groups) and worked with them for thirty years in all, culminating in the position of County President of North Yorkshire.

In 1975 I began to work with Sue Ryder (Baroness Ryder of Warsaw OBE who had married Leonard Cheshire). Since the war, Sue Ryder had taken over large country houses and turned them into nursing homes to care for the sick and disabled people of all ages. I went to visit one such house, Holme Hall at Holme on Spalding Moor near Hull, to see if I could take my St John Ambulance cadets for some practical experience. A very sick man there had suggested that I might be able to help with some fundraising, so I was shown round the home and when they suggested that to convert the billiard room into a kitchen would cost £15,000 I said that I thought the costs would be much higher. They were so surprised to find someone who understood about country houses and real costs. Not long after that, Sue Ryder asked me to set up the first management committee. The next eleven years were very challenging and very rewarding. I worked long hours to motivate people to take an interest in the work we were doing. I gave talks to the general public, to Rotary and luncheon clubs. I had to tell the story of Sue Ryder's life and her work with the SOE (Special Operations Executive) during the war in Poland. I had to tell *her* story with a passion that brought tears to the eyes of many.

It was complicated, draining, fascinating and exasperating. When I first saw the home there was no running water for the nurses, no nurses station and no cups and saucers for the patients that were not chipped. Facilities, equipment and help were minimal. I, literally, opened the doors to the public and showed them and they came to help. Local china painting classes sent us cups that had been lovingly painted. It was a sad day when we had enough money to buy commercial crockery. People turned up to do the flowers, drive the patients on outings, and raise the money. Always just when I needed help, just when I was at my lowest ebb, help walked through the door.

I took Richard and my other children at weekends and they joined in, just as they did when I was camping or on duty with the St John Ambulance.

I was a strong Christian in those days and a regular churchgoer. I learnt that when you really asked for help, in the right way, help was there. I would often turn into the gates of the house, knowing I had a very difficult time ahead that day with difficult decisions to make and I would ask God to hold my hand and put the right words into my mouth. It never failed. I only failed when I did not ask for that help.

There seemed to me an urgency about the work that needed doing at the Sue Ryder Home. There was so much to be done. The kitchens were inadequate, the rooms had to be redesigned to conform to new health standards, the house had to be rewired, the staff pay had to be restructured so that they could be paid monthly into bank accounts instead of paying out cash each week. We built a new physiotherapy wing, with staff facilities above. There were eight elderly French nuns living in the house when I first went there. It had been a convent and there was a beautiful chapel (this was one of the requirements of Sue Ryder). There were seventeen acres of garden and woodland to care for. The only way to improve things, in my opinion was to lead from the front and this was not always popular. In the eleven years I was there we did achieve a lot. We must have raised in excess of one million pounds in that time, which in those days was a considerable sum of money. We developed it from a twenty-four bed unit to forty-five beds with a staff of ninety. It became the second largest Sue Ryder nursing home in the country and was highly respected for its care for people with illnesses such as cancer, motor neurone disease, multiple sclerosis and Huntington's disease. However, its success brought pressure. It had been very difficult to find matrons who could cope with all the changes. We had to find a good bursar to work with the matrons. We found wonderful people but there were reasons why they did not or could not stay. Eventually the staff decided that I had moved too fast for them, achieved too much too quickly and they lined up at the AGM and asked me to go. The final straw had been a matron who they had loved but who had a number of difficulties with other things and we had to give her notice.

I had always said that I would go if anyone felt I should, but I did not expect it to happen in the way it did. I was gutted, it was as if I had been hit in the stomach. It had all been so public. Although I had been given three months to go, I walked out of the home that day and never went back. There was no way could I have faced the staff again if that was how they felt. I felt I had failed and yet so many people had helped us to achieve so much. I had met some wonderful people.

I learnt a great deal from being 'sacked'. I had to move on. I was terribly hurt, but then it was my fault, or was it? What would I do? My confidence went through the floor, as I sought to learn from this experience. Later I learnt that Sue Ryder herself was removed from her own Foundation. Somewhere, somehow the structure of the organization was in a muddle. Sue Ryder had warned me of the need to 'always watch your back'. We had both been caught unawares.

In 1988 we moved to York, I had now given up the Sue Ryder work and most of my other charities. I decided that I would be my own boss for a while and earn my own money. I had years of experience in the voluntary sector and now seemed the right time for me to set up my own fundraising consultancy with help from a local friend. I went to conferences – I love conferences, all the networking and talking and learning. I went to the big national fundraising convention in Birmingham. I was particularly interested in the international lecture on how to raise money from the European Commission. Next stop was Amsterdam at the International Fundraising Convention. This was to prove useful as a few years later, in 1998 I found myself giving one of the lectures at this conference to an international audience of 150 people on how to set up a charity in Thailand. This was following the death of Richard and after my first visit when I decided to set up Karen Hilltribes Trust (KHT). The talk was called "Just Do It"; and that is exactly what I went on to do.

Meanwhile I took on a number of fascinating projects in the art world, with schools, museums and the general development of charities. I took up an appeal to raise £750,000 to rebuild the Lantern Tower at Blackburn Cathedral in Lancashire and was just about to launch it as a Stained Glass Appeal: the day we launched the appeal was the day we buried Richard.

Soon after the funeral I had to go back to work. I had left them to cope for a few days over Richard's funeral and I am pleased to say that we reached our target for the Lantern Tower and the stained glass windows look wonderful.

Chapter Five

Family Illness and Huntington's Disease

In September 1998 a year after I had made my first visit to Thailand to meet with Jim and stay with the Karen people, some very good friends offered us a holiday. This was the greatest possible gift at that time. It had been a fraught year and I was exhausted. We had a happy week. The following week, late one night, Oliver called for help. He could not breathe properly. I called the doctor and she called the 'blue light ambulance' immediately. Oliver was rushed into York hospital where I was told that the right mitral valve in his heart had collapsed and he would need very major, immediate surgery to replace it. The nurses were brilliant. He was moved from ward to ward in preparation for his move to Leeds where the actual operation would take place. It seemed to take several days for them to get everything in place for this major operation but eventually the day came.

Georgina was back in France, Anne was in Australia and David was the only one of my children who could come. David and I met the anaesthetist the night before the operation and with tears in his eyes he told me that it was going to be very difficult to get Oliver through this. It would be touch and go. I can remember thinking that Oliver had had a good life, he was now seventy-two years old and if he was to die, then so be it. I told the anaesthetist that I would quite understand if he did not survive and he should not feel badly because he could only do his best. If he was to die, then it was meant to be.

I went home for a short break. David came with me, but not for long. He was beside himself with worry. He felt compelled to be with his father. Oliver was not going to die! He went back to the hospital to sit with Oliver through the night, just sitting there to be with him. He went with him to the operating theatre and waited outside. He sat by his bed in the intensive care recovery unit almost constantly for two days. Oliver slowly recovered, and was moved to another ward. Anne had come back from Australia to see him and was soon showing him how to feed himself. To give him this new mitral valve in his heart meant taking his body down to freezing point and removing the heart to attach this new valve. It would be a long journey back to health, but with David and Anne to support and encourage, I felt things were improving.

Except for one thing; his physical movements were erratic. He was not walking straight down the hospital corridors and the control of his hands when he was feeding was difficult. There seemed to be a fragmentation of the co-ordination between his head and his hands. The nurses pointed out that he had Huntington's disease. They advised that as soon as Oliver was reasonably recovered, in a few months time, that he should see the consultant and have some tests.

Oliver's mother had been thought to have Huntington's chorea. A chorea means involuntary movements that make it difficult to function. She had needed full nursing care towards the end of her life. She had lived to be eighty-four, but when I first met her in 1963 when she was about seventy, she was having difficulty pouring out the tea, difficulty walking, speaking and problems with her general co-ordination. As time went on, she was referred to specialists who had thought about Huntington's chorea, but there were no tests that could prove it.

Now Oliver seemed to have the same thing, or did he?

The consultant was very kind and understanding. He explained how difficult it was to discover that you have the disease. It would mean a blood test in due course but there would need to be some counselling before that, because it could be so difficult for everyone if he was proved positive. How would it affect the whole family? I remember him telling me that it was one of the worst diseases you could have. It was a long time before I realised what he meant.

Huntington's disease is a progressive, neurodegenerative, hereditary disorder that affects the voluntary and involuntary muscle co-ordination in your body. There is a mutated gene that prevents the brain from operating normally. It affects behaviour, planning, reasoning, rational thinking; it affects how you receive messages in the brain and transfer these messages to your hands and body. As the person continues to live with this genetic mutation, so it becomes more difficult for the person to function. It gradually damages specific areas of the brain including the motor areas and those dealing with executive functions. It can lay dormant until you are older in life, like Oliver and his mother; or you can find that you have the symptoms at a much younger age. The average age is thirty to fifty, and the life expectancy then is five to fifteen years. Some people get it in childhood.

There is a 50:50 chance that your children will have it. It is complicated to describe to anyone, because it can be so different in every person but recently I was told that in Huntington's patients, the genetic code located on chromosome 4 repeats itself too many times which decays certain types of cells faster than is necessary. Different cells in the brain have different resilience to this mutated gene, but as it wiggles its way around the brain it upsets other genes around it, causing havoc and disturbance with physical, mental and emotional activities. There is no medication that will cure the illness, but medication can help improve the functioning of the brain; calming down the erratic movements. This, however, can cause side effects.

If you have it, it affects your mortgage, your insurance, your driving and other important things in your life. You will also, one day, need full nursing care.

It was only in 1993 that it had become possible to isolate the gene and recognize it as Huntington's disease. Until now Oliver's brothers and sister had not thought about it. In their mother it had just been something that happened to her in her old age. Now the consultant wanted to know which other members of his family, going back several generations, might have had something that could now be similar. We had to look at the whole family tree. His grandmother certainly had it although it was thought to be MS at the time.

I had cause to remember my time at the Sue Ryder Home; where there had been a number of people there with it. They were extremely difficult to nurse, their movements and irrational behaviour were difficult to deal with and the nurses needed specialist training.

The consultant was careful to ensure that we had all the facts before we decided to have the test to confirm one way or another as to whether Oliver had the gene. To know that you have the disease can be as difficult as knowing that you have not got it, he said. Not to have it, means that you can lead a normal life but when other members of the family have it, you start to wonder what normality is. To know that you have it will affect everything you do throughout your life. After a year, when Oliver was on the road to recovery from his heart operation, we decided to go ahead with the test.

The day that we learnt that he had inherited the gene, was another turning point. Oliver faced it head on. He decided to talk about it and tell others so that they would understand when there was a problem. He was immediately forbidden to drive a car. We had a moral obligation to inform all his family. His sister was immediately tested and confirmed negative. His brothers felt that they did not want the test. This left just Oliver in his immediate family, knowing that he had it. Now we had to think about the future and to think about our own children.

Georgina, my eldest daughter, had always had co-ordinating issues and behavioural difficulties that had caused me no end of worry. Was this the problem with Georgina? We tried to give her a happy childhood. A country life, a local school, ponies and dogs, but there were always complications. There had been an exaggerated imagination, little rationale and obsessive thoughts. The headmaster of Fangfoss primary school found her imagination exciting, but difficult. She moved to the Mount School in York where the staff found difficulties. She kept falling down the stairs and they asked us to call in a consultant, as it did not seem normal. Tests were done, but to no avail. I was just told to consult my family doctor, if I did not know how to bring her up.

Her teenage years continued to be fraught and when she started work she would lose her bus tickets, could not manage her money, broke machines, dropped trays; all things that other people do from time to time so we just thought that this was her character. Most things that she bought had to be returned to the shop, whether it was new shoes or a vacuum cleaner. She could not be satisfied. Eventually she married and the same issues continued but got worse. These ranged from missed appointments, losing health records and destroying equipment. Confused by emotional and physical difficulties life was difficult for her. She was unable to sort out any problems other than to walk away from them. When she left her husband soon after her second child was born, she moved house every year, making the excuse that other people were the problem. She knew that stress made things worse but somehow she made life even more stressful through her actions. In spite of the fact that she always had a great sense of fun and was a loving person, she could not manage the day-to-day functions of life. When life was difficult, she would discard possessions and move on, usually at very short notice.

After Richard died she had brought her children, Molly (then five years old) and Marcus (aged three years), to live with us. It was a very fraught six months; she was invariably ill and I was left to take the children to school and take her to the hospital; once in the early hours of the morning. Usually there was nothing really the matter. Another time she was admitted at twenty-four hours notice for seven weeks with psychiatric problems, again leaving me with the children. She seemed unable to eat normally, and her behaviour was irrational to say the least. Georgina started training to do Reiki healing and in order to try and earn some money she thought she could set up a clinic in York, but she had no real qualifications and had not worked out the practical details. The day it was due to open the finances were not in place and she was not allowed on the premises.

Oliver just smiled through all the difficulties. He often tried to support her but this just encouraged her to continue down the same irrational routes. About six months after Richard died she inherited some of Richard's money. That very day, she got in the car with her two children, two suitcases and drove to Brighton. From there she moved to London and then to France, all in the space of four months, where she had found a derelict house and thought she would convert it. Instead she had a major operation and I had to go to be with her and look after the children. With Oliver not well at that time in York and Georgina needing three months to convalesce in France, or so the doctors told me, I brought the children back to the UK to look after them for three months.

As she recovered she got a job in France as a waitress and became a French citizen. She made new friends and moved house again and again and again, discarding possessions each time and so the story continued. It was another two years before they confirmed that she had Huntington's disease. Somehow it was a relief to know that she had it. It gave us the answer to so much of her story. I don't know if it helped her to know, although at times it was useful. She could now get special help and would get financial support with the children, with cleaning the house, filling in forms and various housing issues.

She has three children now and we don't know which one of them has it. Life has continued to be strange for her. Desperately wanting a life of fun and unable to sort things out, but still fighting to manage her own affairs, she has no home, no possessions, no money and has had various accidents. In December 2008 there was an even worse car accident than previously, in which she broke three vertebrae in her neck. I visited her in the clinic at Collioure in the south of France on the Spanish border where she spent three months recovering. After seven years living in different places in the Dordogne she now found herself in a small flat in Perpignan. Georgina has since made a remarkable recovery and her spirit continues to be amazing but with no home and no possessions of any sort and with three children in different places, no one knows what will happen next. In 2010 she came home to York and stayed for three months. Where she will ultimately live and how she will cope is something for the future. For now she knows she needs a great deal of support, mentally, physically and financially.

In spite of all the difficulties, Georgina has a great sense of humour and a huge amount of experience which she longs to share with others, but

Footsteps to the Jungle

knows that most people would not understand. She loves people, is creative and has a very beautiful singing voice and to me is a beautiful person.

When Oliver was diagnosed with Huntington's disease, David was about to get married. He felt he should have the test. It might affect his future as to whether he would have children. It was soon confirmed that he too had the gene. It was a real blow and while it was hard for his wife to be; she seemed ready to support him. The thought of knowingly bringing children into the world with a 50/50 chance of Huntington's was difficult. Maybe there would be a cure for it by the time any children were old enough to worry about it? He was later told that they could take out the gene, but that would mean disturbing other genes and there would be the chance of autism or some other problem. They could have IVF, but they wanted *their* baby. He took a chance and Scout was born in 2004. She is a beautiful child but sadly the marriage failed.

Anne still had to decide whether she would have the test. The enormity of the decision was not to be underestimated. No one should go alone to receive the news. If she had it, how would she find a husband? How could she buy a house? When would she show signs of it? Her good friend Laura went with her to learn that she did not carry the gene. The relief was amazing and her whole life took on a new dimension. Now a qualified nurse, she decided to join the army. She went to Sandhurst to go through the officer-training course. The same Sergeant Major, who had looked after Richard, now looked after Anne. It was quite emotional for us but we were very proud. She joined Queen Alexandra's Royal Army Nursing Corps becoming a Captain quite soon after. After a short time in the Gulf, she came back to work at Headley Court the rehabilitation centre for brain injured people and has become a neuro specialist nurse in rehabilitation. A few years later she was found to have thyroid cancer but after the thyroid was removed and she had the radiation treatment there are no longer signs of the cancer.

One thing seemed absolutely sure to me in all of this, that Richard, like Anne, did not have Huntington's disease.

Oliver was still recovering from the huge operation to replace his heart valve. The anaesthetic had taken a lot out of him. Two years later and he was slowly getting stronger. He no longer fell asleep in the car. He talked of playing golf and going to see his brother in Canada or Florida. How was he going to cope with the future, with knowing that he had Huntington's disease? He was told that his problems could only get worse, so he faced it, squarely. He talked about it, so that people understood when he was not coping. He took up exercise to ensure he stayed as fit as possible. He went to see speech therapists to help him with his speech. He employed a trainer to work on his co-ordination and to strengthen his muscles. Then his friends rallied round and took him for lunch at the golf club.

He needed to remain as independent as possible. Independence has been crucial, not just for him but all of us who care for him. In 2010 at the age of eighty-three and with very focused specialist help from a good nurse who worked with him on a one to one basis, Oliver was still able to walk a mile and enjoy the bluebells in the woods, the trees at the Castle Howard Arboretum, the walks around the campus of York university, the friends he met everywhere. His diet and all his activities were very closely monitored. Sadly in August 2010 after a very heavy fall he was transferred to a nursing home.

In the midst of these things my grandson Marcus, then thirteen years old, came to live with us. He had come when Georgina had no settled place to live in France and Marcus was coming up to his time in secondary school. The three years living with us were extremely difficult as he was very bright but found it difficult to integrate. There was no doubt that he missed his mum but somehow it was always difficult to arrange holiday plans with her so he sometimes only saw her twice a year. However this period had made it difficult to find carers for Oliver who could also cope with a teenager such as Marcus. Then in 2008, after the three months in the clinic in Collioure, Marcus went back to live with his mother for a whole year. He had turned his back on his GCSE's and felt he really needed to be with his mum. After a year, the situation had become difficult again and I had to fetch Georgina and Marcus back to York. This time I thought Georgina just might stay in England, but she only stayed a few weeks. She needed to go back to see her nine year old son in the Dordogne. Marcus settled back into school in York a much calmer and more responsible young man. It remains to be seen what happens next.

My life was VERY full. During that time I was discovering so much about Huntington's disease, I would limp from subject to subject, finding that my work in Thailand was far more rewarding and 'pulling' than all the family issues.

Was that selfish? Probably. I was also frustrated and stressed with Georgina as well as Oliver. I was already finding it difficult with all the different things that I had to face. It affected our social life; people began to treat us differently; not to ask us to social occasions. The difference in our ages became difficult. I had to leave him to cope sometimes and he managed, and that was fine. He always understood and gave me great encouragement to 'do my own thing'. Over the years we have learnt how to cope and support each other. My Sue Ryder work had shown me how difficult it can be for relatives of those who are ill and the importance of not getting too close. One needs to keep the respect for each other and see the good things. It was my job to see that he had good care and that his interests were met but not always feel that it had to be me that should be there. Then there were the finances which had to be managed but soon became crippling. Living so close to the university as we do, we have had a wonderful series of young university students, some of whom have worked with us for several years. They have all found Oliver interesting and love his sense of humour. These friends have enriched my life too. Nevertheless I remain very pleased to have Thailand to focus on, an outside interest that has taken me into another world.

Chapter Six

The Richard Worsley
Memorial Project

It was in January 1997, three months after Richard died, that I had another fax from Thailand. A team of young volunteers working with the Karen people deep in the forest had been installing a clean water system. The village had 200 people living there, all Catholic, in stilted houses without any electricity. Several had malaria and typhoid and they were so thrilled to be getting clean water. The fax told me that there was now a large plaque beside the tanks with the words:

Richard Worsley Memorial Project

A deep lump was in my throat. Why was this happening? Then I remembered what Richard had said: "Please Mummy, I hope that one day you will help these people, because they really need your help." Could this be the time? What could I do? I had rather a lot going on in my life. Georgina was still living with us, with Molly and Marcus. I had various charities I was involved with and Oliver was not that well, but somehow this was a 'calling'. I felt I had to do something. So I started by setting up an appeal for £50,000 and immediately wrote to all those who came to Richard's funeral to tell them about this. They started to send me money.

This was when I began to remember about Michael in Oxford. His wife had started the Mae Phon Karen Hilltribe Trust in support of the place at Mae Phon at Mae Klang near Chom Thong. It was a registered charity and Michael was kind enough to agree that we should use this charity although in time we would need to amend the constitution to take account of a wider geographical area.

Now thirty-eight years after my first visit to Thailand on my flight in the Piper Aztec, I was fifty-six years old. It was nine months after Richard died and I decided to set off again to Thailand. I had no idea what I would find and I needed to make contact with a group of volunteers from Gordonstoun School who would be out there installing a water system. In principle I would go to see what had captivated Richard. In July 1997, I set off from Leeds/Bradford airport and then via Amsterdam to get the KLM flight to Bangkok.

As I walked through the airport shops in Amsterdam I suddenly felt Richard pushing me. He seemed to be encouraging me to buy a camcorder. I distinctly remember feeling this pressure. I had to buy a really good camera. Richard would have bought a good one and I knew that I would be using it a lot. I did not realize that there was no electricity in the villages and I might have difficulty charging the batteries. I had to buy these very expensive batteries in Bangkok.

I met up with a professor from Nottingham University who had helped me book hotels and introduced me to Bangkok. He was having dinner with the Ambassador who would be pleased if I joined them.

The next day and already exhausted I set off for Chiang Mai by air. I was met at Chiang Mai airport by Jim. The temperature was forty degrees and the humidity 100 per cent.

Now Jim drove me deep into the forests to find the village of Ban Huay Ku Pa where another water system was to be installed. It was a six hour drive, often through heavy rain until we eventually turned off the tarmac road towards the village. The village had a population of two hundred people (seventy households), all Catholic. There was no electricity or clean water; the only water could be collected from the river and it was very polluted. We drove down the village street; a muddy track with fences on both sides and stilted houses behind. Ahead of us was the Catholic Church and down by the river was the primary school.

Further along was the large wooden house where ten English volunteers were living. They had been working all day in the forests, digging trenches to take the pipes from the water source. It was very hot and humid and they were tired and hungry. The flies and mosquitoes were dreadful and they were everywhere.

A little Karen lady shyly greeted me and took me to see the house they had made available for me. Somsri (her Karen name) was the wife of the headman in the village. Their house had been totally cleared of their belongings (not that they had anything other than a few clothes and their cooking equipment). I went up the high wooden steps to the large room, the only one in the house. The walls were wooden slats with a few inches of daylight between each slat. Next morning the cockerels and the pounding of the rice woke me at 4.30am. There was no protection from mosquitoes or the heat. There was a small tub of water and an enamel plate at the top of the stairs, for me to wash with. They had found a mosquito net and a blanket for me. The pillow was small and hard and made of old blanket material and that was all there was in this large room. Somsri kept coming up the stairs to see if I wanted anything. She escorted me to see other Karen people and I sat with them that evening talking about Richard and how I felt about being in the forests. I did not speak a word of their language, but somehow we could communicate. Salahae, the Karen manager who had known Richard and was working with Jim at the time to design and install the systems, helped to translate, as did Jim when he wasn't busy with the English volunteers and their teacher.

Later that night I discovered the joys of visiting the loo. In the dark, from the stilted house, I had to find my way down the steps, put on some flip flops and with the light of the moon and the stars find my way through the mud to the building where the latrine was. It was just a shack with a door falling off its hinges and inside was a concrete floor with a china squat; a scruffy space where the family came to wash, resulting in a random collection of wet clothes and toothbrushes mostly on the floor or hanging over the wooden edge to the building. Beside the squat was a tub with a scoop to throw water into the hole. No 'facilities for hand washing' but with luck there was a bar of soap. It was raining hard and the mud was very slippery. The forest was quiet and I just hoped all would be okay.

Over the next few days I got used to all this. The rain seldom stopped, the mud was very slippery. The flies and mosquitoes were everywhere and everyone was worried about tummy problems.

One of the Karen died of malaria. I was privileged to sit with the family as they grieved. The coffin was simple; and there was a large crucifix behind the coffin and a small statue of Our Lady nearby. On the coffin were plates of food – rice and spices – to feed the spirits. The coffin was eventually carried on bamboo poles to the burial ground on the side of the mountain in the forest. I followed the funeral cortege of chanting Karen villagers to the hill where the local leaders said prayers. Karen funeral rites are mainly to ensure that the soul (kala) of the deceased will not return to the place of the living. There were no tears as death in life is to be expected.

A few months after I left the village I heard that the headman had been shot. There was some suspicious story about logging and someone had shot him, using him as a scapegoat. He was Somsri's husband, a young man of around thirty-five years old, charming, intelligent and much respected. Now he was dead his house had to be destroyed in order that the bad spirit should be removed and now Somsri would struggle financially.

The young team were away all day, digging trenches and gluing pipes. So I set off to photograph everything I could find. The Karen people did not mind this; they were intrigued by this relatively elderly English woman, so busy with a camcorder, such as they had never seen before. They came with me wherever I went, out of curiosity, but also to make sure I was alright (so I learnt later). Language did not matter; we seemed to understand each other. They seemed to understand that I would come back, but this was not something that I could promise. I just knew that Richard was right and I started to learn why Richard had loved the Karen people so much. I had promised Richard that I would help these people and there was a journey ahead that I would have to follow. Somehow Richard was leading this and there was a story unfolding.

When I returned to the UK I made a promotional video from the footage I had taken. I found a film editor in Hull whose patience was to be tested to its limits. The normal thing would have been to have written a script and then filmed for the script. Not me! I had taken the filming and was now trying to make a story of it. What is more I knew what story I wanted to tell and I spent hours with him being very persistent. I had to be very involved as he cut it and shaped it and I was very fussy.

We had to have a logo and whoever I talked to about that I could not find anything better than the one I had designed. I had a good friend, Howard, who I had worked with as a professional fundraiser for some years and he now came to my rescue again. I bounced every idea at him and he kept me focused. We designed a cover that had to be simple and cheap to reproduce. The video was limited to nine minutes. It told the story of Richard, of the Karen people, the work that was needed and of the volunteers.

The result was that we raised nearly £50,000 in 1997 to support the Karen people. I needed to keep some money in reserve to develop things for the future and I also needed to be absolutely sure how it would be spent if I did send it. Over the next two years I worked with Jim to help him fund various things, but as time went on I realized that I needed to set up a proper charity in the UK with proper reporting and accounting procedures, good controls and appropriate trustees. I could see that I would have to consider a Foundation in Thailand in due course but this would have to come later.

Meanwhile the work was continuing in Thailand. Volunteers were coming to stay in Ban Huay Kai Pa. They would stay for five months to teach English in the primary school. They joined in the everyday life and had a wonderful time. An occasional water system was built but only when funds allowed. Salahae, the Karen who had known Richard, was in charge of this now.

Back in England, I was working from home in a small bedroom that I had turned into an office to cope with all the letters to be answered after Richard's death. Now I would have to move to a larger room as the work increased.

Chapter Seven

Salahae

Salahae was twenty-four years old when he met Richard, then nineteen years old. Richard was just one of several volunteers, but these two people shared a sense of humour and laughed together.

It was Salahae who first asked me to help the Karen people, who now worked with me to "make it all happen". He became part of my life. I had arrived in Thailand after Richard died, not knowing what to expect or who anyone was, but Salahae was the one who stayed in constant touch with me. I spoke with him every week from England.

On my frequent visits to Thailand, it was Salahae who drove me everywhere and we talked and talked about so many things. He would often tell me in his broken English, but with enormous passion, about how he had struggled to have an education, about his adventures, and about how he made enough money to build his own house. The more I heard, the more I felt I needed to record it.

He was born in the village of Ban Huay Khi (Huay Khi means 'little stream') on 15 June 1965. Salahae always refers to this village as his 'was born' village. He was the eldest of eleven children. He was named by his grandmother. '*Sala*' was the name of a good friend who arrived at the house that day. '*Hae*' means 'is coming' or 'hot'. (Salahae). His Thai name is Wichien Bunrachaisawan. As he has Thai citizenship he uses his Thai name at all times except when in the Karen villages and when working with us.

Salahae's father's name is Do Ka Bunrachaisawan. He was born in a border village called Huay Ton Noon in 1943 and was one of five children. He was often sick with typhoid or malaria and to this day suffers from asthma. Salahae's mother's name is Khi Cher. She was born in the area of Ban Huay Khi and was one of three children. His mother worked in the rice fields and was very strong. The village itself moved some time later to the present site. I visited the place where the village used to be, it was only a few miles from the Burma border, deep in the jungle. It must have been a very primitive existence but there was something quite special about living in such a place. Now Ban Mae Khi is a settled village of around 100

Family tree depicting Salahae's father and mother's eleven children

Do Ka Bunrachaisawan (father) — Khi Cher (mother)					
Salahae	Takoo *male, married with two children, living in village*	Bo La *male, living in village*	Pa Bodee *male, trained in Bangkok as a lawyer but returned to his village*	Chaisi *looks after a guest house in Chiang Mai*	Siporn *female, married, teaching in village on the border*
	Pa NooNoo *male, died of cerebral malaria aged eight*	Toopaw *female, died in childbirth, child died later*	Toowa *female, married, lives south of Mae Sariang*	Girl *died as a baby*	Chaepo *killed at the age of twenty-one on a motorbike in Chiang Mai*

people with a large Catholic church, and even this village is twenty kilometres from the small town of Khun Yuam. There is no public transport or means for children to get to school even in 2010. Do Ka's father and mother (Salahae's paternal grandparents) had died when he was fifteen and Salahae's maternal grandmother who had played an important part in Salahae's life died in 2008 at the age of eighty-five. Salahae had made the machete for him that I still have to day.

All the family were Animist until about 1960 when Father Roger Bae de Bideaux came to Ban Huay Ton Noon, the neighbouring village to Ban Huay Khi, his 'was born' village. Late one night, around eleven o'clock, he arrived with a friend. All the villagers except for one old lady ran away because of this big giant of a man who came, obviously to eat them all up! "No," said Father Bae de Bideaux to the little old lady. "I have come to help you. You believe in the spirits and it is very complicated. Animists kill animals and keep blood to give to the spirit. They take the heart and lung for spirits, to say sorry. They think the spirits can heal the sick, but it is not true. You must give up being animist. I have come to tell you about Christianity." Salahae was later to discover that he was a friend of Father Jo from Mae Phon, near Chom Thong, where he was at school.

Salahae remembers very well the day Father Bae de Bideaux came. He was a small boy, aged about three or four. He saw this very tall man arrive and stood transfixed by the size of his nose and big blue eyes. (No Karen or Thai people have blue eyes.) He described it vividly to me, how he had

54

turned his head to the side in amazement at such a sight. It was a European nose the shape of which is quite different to the Karen. It was the first time he had seen a European, and the blue eyes seemed huge.

Salahae grew up, running around barefoot in the mud until at the age of five he went to primary school in the 'police border' school in Ban Huay Ton Noon. This meant getting up at 4.30 every morning to leave home at 5.30 for the seven kilometres walk to school. Often during the rainy season it just rained all day. Always barefoot, he and a few friends would return at 6.30 each night. In his first year he had a slate and charcoal to record his lessons. It was important to learn quickly as the information would be washed off at the end of each day. In his second year he was given a pencil and a notebook. The teachers were also members of the police force, whose job it was to protect the border, and they were often called to issues on the border. If there were problems the teachers would have to suddenly leave the classroom and would often be gone the whole day.

In those days there were tigers. The tigers would come into the village at night and steal the animals. One day they knew the tiger was coming, but in the night the dog needed to go for a pee. So his father put a rope round the dog and had to lower the dog through the floor of the house, so that he could quickly pull him up again if the tiger came. There are still a few tigers, but not many. In 2008, a tiger came and took six buffalo from the village.

There were bears too. There still are a few bears but they are to be feared because they will fight humans. Salahae was eighteen and remembers one incident well. He had come home from Chiang Dao School for two weeks holiday and was helping his family with their various jobs. In the evening his father went to the forest to collect vegetables and met a bear with a baby. The bear bit hard into Do Ka's thigh and damaged his finger too as he tried to escape. His finger has remained bent all his life and he still has the scars of four teeth on his right thigh. At the time there was a lot of blood. Salahae was not far away and heard the cries for help. They had to carry his father the five kilometres to Huay Ton Noon. They had tied his clothes around the wound to make a tourniquet, relatives lent them a motorbike and then they found a pickup to take them to Khun Yuam hospital. The hospital said they could not deal with such things and sent him an hour north to Mae Hong Son.

Salahae remembered another story about his childhood, about when he wanted to go fishing with his friends. They had a fishing line with a hook but he had no money to buy one for himself, so he found a rope. He shrieked with laughter as he told me what happened next. He found a bamboo beetle, these beetles have a very big leg which is sharp so they can hang onto the bamboo while they lay their eggs. Their legs are very strong. Salahae collected the beetles and legs and made a hook. He put a worm on the end of the beetle leg hook. He was very excited about this but sadly he never caught a fish because the leg straightened out with the weight of the worm and dropped off. It was a source of great amusement to him and his friends. He then explained this to his grandmother and asked if he could borrow a pin, and bent it to make a hook. He then went down to the river again, but it was the rainy season and the river was swollen. He got his hook stuck in the rocks. He was very scared in case the crocodiles or snakes came. He wanted to pull the hook out of the rocks but it broke. Now he had no hook and he cried all the way home but Salahae laughed his infectious chuckle, as he finished his story.

At nine years old, Salahae moved to Mae Phon, 75 kms east of his home village. Mae Phon is a small village near Mae Klang twelve kilometres north of Chom Thong and an hour west of Chiang Mai. So many years later Richard stayed in Mae Phon. I too visited this village with Jim.

Mae Phon was run by Father Jo, a French priest. Father Jo had been sent from France as a missionary, and was a friend of Father Bae de Bideaux. He had initially been to China but then went to Burma. There he met two Karen people who taught him English. They brought him into Thailand and thence to Chom Thong. Father Jo decided that Chom Thong was not the right place to set up a 'centre' or community for the Karen people. He found his way to Mae Phon which at that time was once owned by Thai lowland people. What is now the village square was the rice fields but the Thai people would not work in the rice field, as they got sick. They thought there must be bad spirits there, so they sold the land to Father Jo.

The school day started early. The children had to collect the bamboo shoots from the forest and the firewood for cooking. There were seventy children to be fed, and they had two meals a day at 8.00am and 4.00pm, paid for by Father Jo.

The first time he went there, his father took him to Ban Nong Haeng from where he would get a lift on the next step of the journey. This was a large village on Route 108, just south of Khun Yuam on the main road south to Mae Sariang and on to Chiang Mai. His father gave him 20thb (£1.00) to last him for the whole year. From there he travelled on a buffalo lorry for seven hours. He had a friend the same age to keep him company. He just took a change of clothes but he still had no shoes. The buffalo lorry dropped him off at Chom Thong and the two friends then walked the twelve kilometres north to Mae Phon. The school year starts in May and it was four months later that he came home for the half-year break. He travelled the same way home but stayed just one week before he returned to finish the year in March. This routine went on for the next two years.

One day, on his way back home from Khun Yuam, when it was very late at night, he discovered he had no money to get help, so he had to walk all the way home by himself. When he got to the big river it was very dark, and there was no bridge. Salahae was frightened to stay there all night, so he took his clothes off and swam across at midnight. He was about fifteen years old. His father was very angry with him and said how dangerous and silly he had been, but Salahae said there was no other way as he had to get home.

He had another fortunate escape when he walked through the forest. One day he had trodden on what he thought was a twig, but it was a snake. He then thought a thorn had pricked him, but the snake had bitten him twice and there were four holes in his skin. There was a man ploughing with buffalo nearby who ran very fast to the village to get some wire to make a tourniquet. Salahae had to keep walking very fast to keep the swelling from getting any worse. In fifteen minutes all the villagers were there and worried. They had to hurry to get help and they made a hammock from blankets and carried him the five kilometres to Huay Ton Noon. There he was put on the back of a motorbike, down a very narrow track all the way to Khun Yuam hospital, a further fifteen kilometres.

Father Jo had asked Salahae if he wanted to join the church. Chiang Dao would be the next step in teaching him about the Catholic faith and priesthood.

At twelve years old Salahae moved to school in Chiang Dao north-east of Chiang Mai where he stayed for two years. To get to Chiang Dao was difficult. Usually he would have to walk the first twenty kilometres through the forest to Khun Yuam where he got the bus. This meant setting off up the high mountain just outside his house. His father pointed him in the right direction and off he went. Although the forest is a myriad of paths, once he had been shown the way he always remembered for the next time. Once he had to walk the whole way and this took him a whole week on foot through the forest.

Salahae had his first pair of shoes, his flip-flops, at the age of twelve. He was away from home for four or five months at a time, with one change of clothes and his school uniform. He still had no money, so he had to work hard to help in the school. His job was to unblock the toilets and empty them when they got too full; as these were just holes in the ground it meant digging the effluent out into sacks and taking it away into the forest. Sometimes he would help the priests, at other times he had the vegetables to prepare for meals. Sometimes there was cement to mix when building work had to be done. Salahae's day was always very long and busy.

Salahae was always top of his class in the lessons and was proving a good pupil. At the age of fourteen Salahae finished primary school and wanted to go and study in Chiang Mai for his secondary schooling. His friends were moving to the Montfort school, which was run by the Congregation of St Gabriel, but it was expensive and Salahae had no money.

So Father Jo had arranged for Salahae to go to secondary school with seminary training in Ratchaburi, near Bangkok. Here the school took all Salahae's possessions from him (not that he had much anyway) but they looked after him for the next six years. He went home once a year, occasionally he would go twice but never for very long. The school was also a commercial college, so it was here that he learnt about business and accounting procedures. Later when I first knew him, his accounts were always beautifully handwritten and exact. He learnt Latin and he was always top of the class. They still wanted him to become a priest, but Salahae said he wanted to help his people in another way. He really wanted to go to university, but he had no money.

He finished at the commercial college at the age of twenty-one and went back to Chiang Mai to get a job. He wanted to be a soldier, but his mother said no. Maybe he could join the border police? But, again, his mother said no. She thought he would soon die if he joined the police, as someone would kill him. She wanted him to be a teacher, but this time it was Salahae who said no.

Desperate to earn some money, Salahae asked his father to lend him 3000 baht (£50) to buy some honey. Honey is wonderful in northern Thailand. The bees make hives very, very high in the trees and collect the pollen from the mountain flowers. They say it is the purest honey in the world. The bears love it and they say the bears have the strongest bones in the world, because of the honey. Salahae bottled the honey and took it to Chiang Mai to sell. He had nowhere to live in Chiang Mai so he lived free in the priest's house and managed to sell two or three bottles a day for 100 baht (£1.50). This gave him a profit of 30 baht. After two weeks he had sold so much that he was able to repay his father and had some money of his own.

Father Jo had heard that Salahae was selling honey and said he was not to sell any more. "You are an ex student now and you must come back and teach at Mae Phon and do a proper job." As Salahae did not have any other work at the time, he went to Mae Phon in 1986 for one year. He had never wanted to be a teacher, but it was a good experience. Salahae always enjoyed his work with the children and was very involved with everything. However, culturally the Thai teachers said this was not acceptable and that he should not be so involved with the children. The teachers had to remain separate, but Salahae did not want to live like that and so he left.

He got a job in a bank in Chom Thong; although sixty people had applied for the job Salahae got it. He had passed all his exams and was doing well.

Life went on and in 1987 Salahae still had very little money. Life in the countryside was changing, chemicals were introduced into agriculture bringing new pollution issues. This brought about a growing need for potable clean water systems in the villages as the rivers became more polluted. It was at this time that Jim was becoming more involved with the Karen people and trying to build clean water systems and Salahae began to help him together with Chompon.

At twenty-four years old Salahae needed transport and the most useful form of that was a motorbike. He had been earning 4,000thb (£60) a year as a teacher and he had saved a little which meant he could put down a deposit on a motorbike. He then needed to buy some land because he knew that he could make more money on the land, so he asked his father to help. His father sold two buffalo and with the money from the sale of his motorbike he was able to put down a deposit on some land. This meant he now had no bike. However, he was starting to earn about 1,000 thb a year and later was able to put down a deposit on another bike. One year on, he sold the bike and was able to repay his father.

Thinking ahead for his future, he wanted to buy better land, nearer to the town where there would be good schools for the time when he would marry and have children. What could he do, he had no money? The cost of land was high and there would be a tax to pay, probably around 80,000 thb in all. So he went to see his father again. "Oh, very interesting," said his father "but I don't have that kind of money." The next year the value of the land had gone up to 100,000thb.

So Salahae thought again " If I wait, I will waste my time". At that time there was a Government policy to lend people money through the Thai Farmers Bank to help with agriculture. So he sold his bike for 20,000 thb and went to persuade his father to take out the Government loan, which as the head of the family he could do. His father said it would be better to buy cheaper land outside the town, and then we don't need to borrow so much money. Salahae pointed out: "No, I am single and I need to prepare for married life. I will pay you back, like before." So his father borrowed the money and he bought the land on which he has now built his own house. The next year the land was valued at more than three times the original price.

Two years later, at the age of thirty, he married Bo who was eighteen years old. She came from the nearby village of Ban Mae Pattana and is one of eight children.

It was in 1997, that Salahae and Bo had their first baby, a girl called Fi. On my second visit to Thailand in 1999, I learnt that their second child, a boy, was desperately ill with malaria. His wife had contracted malaria while pregnant and the baby was transferred to Mae Hong Son hospital but died at three months old. There was a big memorial service in the Catholic Church in Khun Yuam and Salahae had placed a large photo of Richard under the altar to ensure he was not forgotten and to say thank you for all the help that came. Jokasee, a boy, was born in 2003. He looks to be strong and intelligent like his father.

Now, in 2010, Salahae has not only built his own house and has two children, but also a large orchard growing lychee fruit trees, some thirty cows and is the district representative of Mae La Noi on the Mae Hong Son Provincial Parliament. He is the first Karen MP to take up this position while not actually living in the district. He lives in the district of Khun Yuam. By the age of forty-four, he hopes to complete a Masters degree in Public Administration at Chiang Mai University in 2011.

Chapter Eight

The Karen Hilltribes Trust and the Foundation for Karen Hilltribes in Thailand

Since my first visit to the Karen people in 1997, I had been working with Jim to raise funds for the clean water systems, but until I had a proper registered charity I could not really move forward.

Then in September 1999 I got an urgent letter from Thailand. Salahae, who I had met in 1997, wrote to me asking for help. He knew I was hoping to set up an independent charity but this request for help was just what I needed to go forward. He wrote: "We just need help for a few years and then we can help ourselves." He went on to say: "We can do so much for ourselves but we need the expertise and funding to make it all happen". Somehow this was all in line with what Richard had asked me to do.

So, in October 1999 I set off for Thailand for the second time since Richard died. Jim met me and he took me to the village of Huay Kong Paw where the water system had been dedicated to Richard. On my first visit it had been too muddy to get there as the village was cut off in the rainy season. Now was my chance to see the sign that was dedicated to Richard.

This village was very high in the mountains with only a dirt track winding through amazingly beautiful and very tall bamboo and teak forests with steep ravines down to the rivers. The village was split into two; one half was Catholic and the other was Baptist. They gave me a warm welcome and some food.

It was a big surprise to find that Jim had organized for an elephant to carry me down the mountain. This huge beautiful animal with a local Karen mahout was waiting beside the Karen stilted house. The house was so high that the elephant could come alongside it for me to climb on from the living area. Then very carefully and very slowly I was taken to the water source, deep in the forest. Very carefully this gracious beast wound her way through deep jungle and high bamboo, along steep slopes to the water source, the mahout cutting the bamboo down as we went to make way for us. Then it was a long four-hour journey to the next village down the mountain track to where there was a road. I shall never forget this journey. Gently swaying with the movement of the elephant, completely trusting, able to look and listen to the forest sounds, it was beautiful.

The real purpose of this visit was to spend time with Jim trying to persuade him of the need to formalize and structure a charity; the need for accountability and good reporting mechanisms; the need for transparency and the need for sustainability. Sadly, much as I admired Jim and much as he wanted initially to work with me, it was soon apparent that Jim and I would not be able to achieve this together. After a lot of discussion Jim and I decided to part company. He wished me luck and agreed that Salahae should work for me. Looking back I don't think there was a way round this.

Salahae and I had been travelling together for the past two weeks. We had talked and talked and talked. He had a vision. I learnt a lot about his vision for the Karen people. He had a passion to help them to build a better future. I learnt a lot about him. Coming from a deep understanding derived from his own childhood and work, he knew what needed to be done. And for all that he came from a simple village life, he also seemed to understand the wider world, the business and charity world; the importance of keeping it small; of what can happen when charities grow too big, of the difficulties of bringing in total strangers who asked so many questions and still may not understand. I talked to him about the needs of the Karen people. Although Salahae had spent most of his time over the past few years installing water systems it was essential that we broadened out the help but always focused on helping them to help themselves. I needed to be sure that several people felt the same way as Salahae.

Then I received the following letter:

Letter from the Karen people
Dated 16.01.2000

From Aksorn (respresenting the Karen people)
Boonmuang (respresenting the Karen people)

To: Penelope
(sic)

We know Penelope about three years ago. She is very kind person. She loves the Karen hilltribe peoples. She helped the Karen peoples a lot past three years. Until now she is trying very hard to carry on helping the poor Karen people who lives too far away from the town. All the Karen peoples are waiting for the helping everyday. The Karen peoples asked the projects through us. Then we asked through Salahae who worked for Penelope always. So we are replace to the Karen peoples said that, thank you very much to Penelope.

Also we never forget Richard Worsley, Penelope's son. He used to be the volunteer for helping the poor Karen peoples in the north of Thailand about six month. He is very friendly, very kind and very helpful to the Karen people. The Karen peoples never forget him too. When he left from Thailand about six years ago. The Karen peoples are waiting him for coming back to help us sometimes. But he died by the accident about four years ago. The Karen peoples are very sad. Because they lost the very kind people, but they also never forget him too.

We are waiting for the long term helping from you. It is not shorter than five years. After that we might can help ourself some. Because we need to help the basic system and very important for our life in the remote mountains are as following:

1) Stream water projects and latrine project
2) Small irrigation project (help the farmer in the rice fields)
3) Education project (help a good students have opportunity
4) Animal bank project (turn the capital after 5 years time)
5) Rice bank project
6) Blankets projects (some peoples they don't have any blankets)
7) Food project (help the student from remote village)

The northern Thailand Karen hilltribe. There are 2000 villages, 400,000 peoples. They are Thai 100% in Mae Hong Son province (all Karen here have Thai ID). They are always thinking of you, you are very important people for them. They are never forget you for ever.

We are so sorry a very poor English. Thank you very much. God blesses you forever.

Love in God.

Signed Boonmuang and Aksorn

So, listening to what the Karen people were saying and with the help of my good friend Howard who had worked with me for many years in the charity sector, we decided to focus on 'Building a Better Future' with the following aims:

1. Improve health by installing clean water systems and latrines
2. Improve access to education with transport, food and accommodation.
3. Improve opportunities for income generation.

I came back to England and registered the charity with the Charity Commission in December 1999. Four years later we amended the Scheme and registered as a company limited by guarantee.

The Karen Hilltribes Trust was up and running! With Richard's picture on the back of every leaflet and our focus on 'Building a Better Future' through improving health, education and income generation, we communicated this to all our friends and I began to give talks to the general public. Most of the trustees were ex-volunteers and some had known Richard.

I had to plan with Salahae as to where we would have our office and how the communication would work between us, when I was based in the UK. I had paid his salary since 1997 so he could continue to install the water systems and work with the volunteers. Now I gave him a fax machine, we spoke every week. Although I had raised money since Richard died, by the time we registered the charity, we had spent virtually all of the money raised on clean water systems. I was under pressure from people in Bangkok to employ an English retired engineer to 'manage' Salahae, but this did not last very long. They had wondered how a middle-aged English woman such as I, living in the UK with a busy life, would ever be able to control or understand what went on in Thailand, not least with the Karen people. Without control there would be all kinds of problems not least with the way money was spent.

It was unfortunate that this man did not take the trouble to understand the way the Karen people were working. He was quick to have his own ideas, to tell Salahae that the tanks should have slanting roofs for instance, but there were plenty of reasons why these ideas could not work in the forests. I then discovered he had a heart problem and could not really get around in the mountains and see what was really happening, so he left. This was quite a challenge. I took seriously the concerns voiced in Bangkok, the need for Salahae to have support in the area; but I knew he had good friends and I had no real worries. I met with the governor of the Mae Hong Son province who was very supportive. I felt we should trust Salahae. I would come out to Thailand at least once, if not twice a year. Volunteers would also come. There would be enough people to ensure that things were running smoothly. His business training and his integrity were valuable assets. He did the accounts monthly, by hand, and faxed them to me where we checked them over against money sent. He never made a mistake. Our long-term aim was to train up a team of Karen, but for now, we had Salahae.

We needed to establish a geographical area. Salahae's home was in Khun Yuam and we used his house as an office, so this became our operational

Penelope aged two with her father on his return from the desert

Oliver and Penelope on their wedding day in 1966

Georgina, David, Penelope with Anne, Richard, Oliver

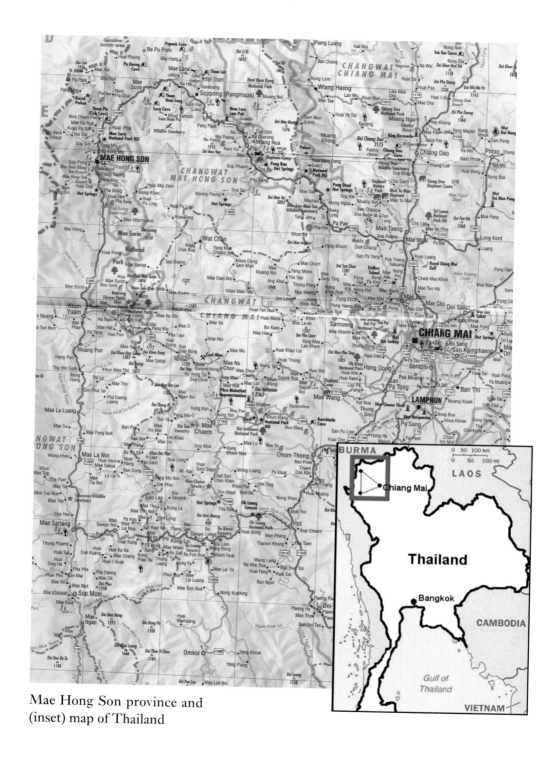

Mae Hong Son province and
(inset) map of Thailand

A local friend

Returning from fishing in the river

Old Karen lady

Man cutting bamboo

Oliver visiting the Karen in 2004

Karen granny with child

Clean water and no more typhoid

Fetching the logs for the fire

Richard visiting a village in 1990

Remote Karen house in 2009

Rice fields in June

Rice planting

Penelope sorting the rice

Pounding the rice

Weaving on a strap loom

Group of Karen women and children

Irrigation project. Water is channelled from river to the fields in canals

Newly regenerated land

Constructing water tanks

Volunteers celebrating the completion of a water system

Old dormitory at Huay Kai Pa

Children outside new dormitory in Huay Kai Pa

Tap–tapping the silver into shape

Making jewellery in their garden

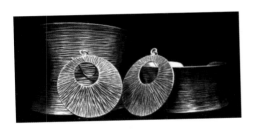

Examples of jewellery made by the Karen people

Chi with his harp

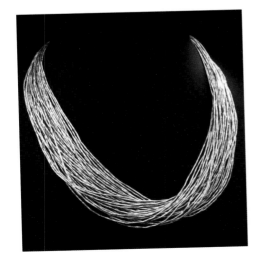

'Hello' in Thai, Karen and English

His Majesty King Bhumibol Adulyadej with Khru Ba

The temple at Wat Prabaht Huay Tom

HQ. Salahae and I discussed how far away we could work. If funds could be raised there was no real reason why we could not go as far away as Mae Chaem, or 50kms south to Mae Sariang and up to Mae Hong Son. This was around 100 square miles. There were hundreds of villages and thousands of people, all needing help. Many villages were cut off in the rainy season and the need was great.

By early 2000 the controls were in place. We only had £4,000 in the bank. Not enough money for us to really get started. We needed to buy a 4WD vehicle for Salahae so that he could get around the villages in the remote mountains. He had to borrow his cousin's car and use motorbikes for the first few months, so that he could keep in touch and find out which villages needed clean water. We did not have any money to buy pipes or equipment for the water systems. Salahae just had to keep in touch with the Karen and wait for us to raise some more money. In June 2000 we took the big leap to buy a 4WD pickup truck, on hire purchase, and we were in business. Then a wonderful donor gave us the money to install a water system.

Meanwhile young people were finding me and asking if they could go as volunteers to live with the Karen people and teach in the schools, just as Richard had done. We sent several volunteers to teach and also to help Salahae with installing a system. They came back thrilled with the enormous challenge they had faced. We had no 'staff' to supervise them. They just had to get stuck in, deal with what they found and cope, they had to make the most of whatever they did. They had to find the way round problems. It was a wonderful training ground for future life. They discovered how the Karen people cope without possessions or money, told others of their experience and in turn they asked to go.

Each volunteer raised money for their own expenses and then each person also raised money to help the children or the village with whom they were more closely involved. This meant they were more likely to take an interest in what they did and we were all helping each other to help the Karen people. Where appropriate, we also asked them to help in Salahae's office with translations or typing.

At home I was running to keep up with the enthusiasm. Money came in, people asked to get involved, and I took on a secretary part time. I moved from communicating with a fax machine, to learning about emails. Unable to afford much outside help I relied on good friends to sort out the computer problems. Toby, a linguistic student from York university, spent hours patiently working with me in my determination to design a website 'in-house'. He became so involved that he remains a regular donor. My days were busy and seldom over before 1.00am. There were reports to write, talks to give to local luncheon clubs, Inner Wheel, Rotary, churches, Women's Institutes; in fact anyone who would listen. First I told them the story of Richard. In order to raise money I had to be able to talk sensibly about the difficulties the Karen people faced, about the climate, the growing of the rice, the devastation of the rainy season, how few children ever went to school because they just did not have the money for the bus fare or they lived too far away. I had to explain it all to the English public and this meant using photography. I had to go to Thailand twice a year to see Salahae, set up projects with him, visit the villages where he wanted to install water systems and again once they were complete. Everywhere I went I took pictures. So did the volunteers and our library was growing.

It is a long journey from England to Thailand. You fly overnight to Bangkok and then up to Chiang Mai. Then you need to spend at least two nights in Chiang Mai to recover from the long flight. It is another day's journey to Khun Yuam, where Salahae lives and from where we could visit the villages. I was exhausted when I set off from Leeds/Bradford airport, so I was absolutely shattered by the time I got to the villages, but there was no time to think about that. I would only have a week, sometimes ten days, and so much to see. It was hot, humid. I would sometimes sleep in a Karen house on the floor, waking to the call of the chickens at 4.30am or the pounding of the rice. My body ached all over, but this seemed slight in the face of the work to be done and things to be seen.

Each journey that I made, I had to stop in Bangkok and meet people. I did not know more than a few people, but I had to find more. For the charity to succeed, our work in northern Thailand needed the support of people in Bangkok. Everywhere I went, people seemed amazed that I was involved in all this, as a result of Richard's death. For a young man from England to have come to help the Thai Karen was wonderful, but for his mother to continue this work after he had died, it seemed, was even more touching.

One contact quickly led to another. My early years had taught me to network. Now it was easy, particularly as the hospitality and friendship in Thailand made sure there was an invitation waiting for me. Whenever I arrived I made a call and was immediately invited round, straight off the plane, I knew I would be welcome. I went to previews, concerts, dinner parties, and meetings. I met all kinds of people. There is quite a large number of expatriots and the British Women's Group were quick to invite me to speak. Gale Bailey was chairman at the time. Even at short notice they found a space for me at their luncheon meetings and gave me the opportunity to give the latest news about my visit to the projects. Soon they were raising money for a water system and since then they have bought blankets and mosquito nets and repaired a dormitory. There were other expatriot organizations such as the St George's Society and BCTFN (British Foundation in Thailand for the Needy) who all gave us donations to support clean water projects, dormitories or blankets and mosquito nets. Wherever I went people were very surprised with what I was doing and when they realized what we were achieving they wanted to be involved in some way. I began to get to know more people and the support came. On my second visit in 1999 I only had two people I could ring. Within a week I knew twenty people. Each journey to Thailand took up nearly three weeks of travelling, meeting, and visiting with virtually no break. However, it was wonderfully rewarding and I came back to raise more money and find new volunteers.

Then there were the hotels. One of our volunteers had contacts in the Conrad Hotel in Bangkok. They offered me accommodation on my visits and eventually took such an interest that they sponsored the running of a dormitory for eighty children for a whole year (see Appendix re Huay Kai Pa dormitory). Every single hotel guest was given information about the charity on the card which housed their room key, and automatically 100 baht was taken off their account unless they specifically asked for this not to happen. We were very grateful indeed and I gave a talk to all the hotel staff.

There were also the backpackers. Thanks to our website, a tour company in Bangkok who brought backpackers from Australia approached me out of the blue. For every backpacker they sent to Thailand they would like us to have 120 baht. Wonderful ... there are lots of backpackers and this has proved a very useful undemanding income for us, especially as we don't see the backpackers as they want to go white water rafting and do touristy things.

Suddenly I found that the press were interested and before long I was being interviewed for a major article in the *Bangkok Post*. Salahae came down from the north because of course it is a project for the Karen people and it was he who needed to talk about the needs of the Karen, not me. Not long after this, I had a call from the *Readers Digest* in Bangkok. They would like to do a major story that would go worldwide. They would send a reporter from France to visit the places that Richard went to and they would follow my journey, talking to the people who first met me in the remote village of Huay Ku Pa. Then they sent a photographer to travel with me on my next visit. The story appeared throughout Asia and part of Europe. It was eventually printed in the UK although the story had been sadly changed. Nevertheless this led to more interest and before long I was interviewed on Radio 4 in England. Other newspapers were interested; I had a story to tell that people wanted to hear.

Other things began to happen. Through various introductions I met with David Thompson, the only English man to have a Michelin star for Thai food. He came from Australia and now had the Nahm restaurant in London. On a previous visit to Thailand he had met with a Karen person who he had much admired. So when approached for an autographed copy of his book as a raffle prize he began to take an interest. He came up to my home in York to see where the charity was based and convinced himself that we were worth supporting. He then decided to make a visit to northern Thailand to walk with the Karen people in the forests and learn what vegetation they collected to use for cooking. He subsequently wrote an article for the *Financial Times* with the heading Grandma's Gin with Lizard Curry (see Appendix 4).

In 2004 I decided to take Oliver. I was travelling with others including the then chairman of the Trust, David Smith, and felt I had enough support to ensure Oliver had someone with him all the time. We stopped in Bangkok for a few days and travelled up to see Salahae. We managed to take him to a remote village and Salahae helped him across the swing bridge to have tea with the Karen people in their stilted house. He loved it (see photo).

Having set up the charity in the UK, there was still one problem. We needed the support of the Thai people. The Karen people that we are working with, all have Thai ID. Their home after all is in Thailand. We needed to raise funds in Thailand and we needed to use the Thai banks to transfer funds. The time was right to set up a Foundation in Thailand. Once again I was stepping into unknown territory. Thai law? Thai charities? Thai banking? At the British Embassy, I met with Peter Comerford who introduced me to his old (young) friend Julia Virulchanya. "Julia is the very person you need," he said. Julia was 100 per cent British with dual nationality. Having spent all her life in Thailand, she spoke fluent Thai, was married to a Thai, had an ordered mind and a good sense of humour. We made friends and it is always fun to come back to Bangkok and I look forward to our Mai Tai (rum punches) together. Peter helped me to find a lawyer, Khun Boonlert, and an accountant, Khun Teerapong. They had both helped with the British Embassy charity and I am grateful for their ongoing support.

To set up a charity in Thailand that is tax effective is not easy. First you have to make sure that the aims of the charity fit in with the ethos of the Thai people. The Thai Foundation was going to have to work under the direction of us in the UK, so it had to have similar aims, but there were small adjustments to be made. The Trustees (Directors) had to have Thai ID, but I was to be President. I had to personally visit and be vetted by the Thai authorities for this position. A year later we were delighted that M.R. Sukhumpand Paribatra agreed to be our chairman. It took two years to get all the documents in place and register the Foundation, but under Thai rules the Foundation would have to prove itself as a well-run organisation before it could become tax effective. This process would take several more years. Then we had to set up a Thai bank account. Banks don't operate in quite the same way in Thailand as they do in the UK. There were also new regulations coming in regarding money laundering and all this needed to be understood. One thing was sure; any money that was in the charity account in Thailand would never be allowed out of Thailand. If anything happened to the charity all the property and money would then belong to the King.

The Foundation for Karen Hilltribes in Thailand has the same aims and objectives as the UK. A memorandum of understanding was written to set out the structure between the Thai Foundation and The Karen Hill Tribes Trust. The ultimate authority would remain in the UK. When the money started to come into Bangkok from various events we could actually fund projects directly from there. This made it much better for donations from Australia and Hong Kong as they could be paid directly into Thailand. Although we were basically supporting the similar projects, the accounts for the Foundation were subject to Thai accountancy law and could not take into account any funds raised in the UK. Likewise the UK Charity Commission could not take into account any funds that went into the Foundation accounts in Bangkok. It became difficult to join the two together in business terms. Thankfully as time has moved on so we have been able to consolidate the accounts each year, but it is not straightforward to explain this to the funders.

Now in 2010, we have a sound structure, and the hope is that we can strengthen our base in Bangkok, slowly, which will take a little pressure off us in the UK.

Having worked with the Karen people for twelve years, our records show that in 2010 we are now helping around 50,000 people in 360 villages. Sometimes just in a small way such as sponsoring a student to university or supplying some mosquito nets, but in others we have installed clean water systems, provided irrigation and built or repaired dormitories. We have a big New Holland tractor which is used to put land back into production, giving people the chance to grow their own crops. All this work has given us a personal and privileged knowledge of 100 square miles of north-west Thailand and the lives of the Karen people under the leadership of Salahae and his team. Our primary project remains clean water, after which their lives will change and the village economy can grow. Education remains high on the list, but there are still seventy per cent of children who do not complete their secondary education because they live too far away and don't have the money for books, transport or accommodation; often not even for the food while they are away.

Salahae is ably helped by a young Karen girl called Nootsabar. Nootsabar came from the first village I ever stayed in and later we sponsored her through university where she studied Business Administration. She now works full time looking after all the administration and documentation for the projects and volunteers.

*   *   *   *

Somehow I had acquired a new family, a large family of many thousands of people, but I still had so much more to discover about the Karen people. Where did they really come from? What was their history? What gave them strengths to cope? What would I learn from all this and how would it change me?

*   *   *   *

Part II

Chapter Nine

From the Gobi Desert to Thailand – the Karen People

I am not bold enough to attempt more than an overview of the history of the Karen people, particularly as it seems that so many people in Asia and Europe, including some very erudite academics, have varying views and thoughts. The Karen people are "much studied". However as time moves on, so their lives are changing even as I write this book, but for now I will tell you what I have found out on my travels.

It would seem that the Karen came through Tibet and Indo China and maybe from the Gobi desert in Mongolia a thousand years ago or more. The mountain ranges and the Salween river run north to south from Tibet to the Andaman and South China seas. The people seemed to migrate south from the harsh environment in Tibet to the warmer and richer lands of Burma and Thailand. The more I listen to people and read about the Karen people their history gets more complicated. Some say they came from Jerusalem and others say they came from China. It is thought there were Karen ministers at the court of Pegu in lower Burma as early as in the 1740s while it is not absolutely clear when they came to Thailand. They certainly settled in Burma for a long time and today number around eight million. In Thailand they are the largest of a number of ethnic hilltribes, numbering around four hundred thousand.

Some say there are fifteen different hilltribe groups in Thailand, but of those most prominent are the Karen numbering around 400,000, the Hmong (Meo), the Lawa, Lisu and Lahu with the Akha being the smallest at around 50,000. The Hmong have entered Thailand mainly since the Second World War, sometimes fleeing persecution in Southern China, North Vietnam and Laos.

Each has its own culture, its own costumes, its own language. They seldom intermarry. The Karen use birth control, but I understand this is not the case with others.

The Karen constitute a puzzle in many ways. The traditions of the Karen would confirm that they come from another land. There is much in their story that is mystical and linked to other places. The most striking story is that of "Htaw Meh Pa", the mythical founder of the Karen race, who lived with his numerous family in some unknown land to the north where their fields were ravaged by a great boar. The patriarch went out and killed the boar; but when the sons went to bring in the carcass, they could find only one tusk which had been broken off in the fray. The old man made a comb out of this, which surprised them all by its power of conveying eternal youth to all who used it. Soon their country became overpopulated and they set out to seek a new and better land. They travelled together till they came to a river called in Karen "Hti Seh Meh Ywa" (the River of Running Sand). Here the old man became impatient at the long time it took the members of the family to cook shellfish and went on ahead, promising to blaze his path that they might follow him through the jungle. After a while the Chinese came along and told them how to open the shells to get out the meat; and then, having eaten, they followed the old man, only to find that the plantain stalks he had cut off had shot up so high that it seemed impossible to overtake him. They therefore settled down in the vicinity. The patriarch went on, taking with him the magic comb which has never been discovered to this day.

Some say that this reference to the River of Running Sand might suggest that they came from the Gobi desert, but I am not sure how much evidence there is to back this up. It could on the other hand, refer to the Yellow River of China. From here they came through Hunnan and into Tibet. The Sgaw Karen are known as the Pga-gan Yaw and this name is derived from one of the four ancient tribes of China. There are two other branches of the Karen known as the Po (red) and Bwe (black) Karen. Each with their own language.

In Thai, predominantly Buddhist, society there was the occasional tendency to regard those of a lower social and economic stratum as being inferiors, principally because their situation stemmed from a lack of 'making merit in their last life'. Fortunately as the years have gone by, this theory is becoming less applicable.

Western Chiangmai and Maehongson consist of mountainous regions with large areas of forest, where Northern Thai and Tai Yai settlements are usually located along the intersecting main river valleys.

The Karen traditionally lived at what is termed the "middle level" in the mountains, namely between 800 and 1,800 metres. The Hmong traditionally lived higher in the hills, partly to facilitate the climatic and altitude requirements of opium production, and partly because this is where this group always preferred to live. Now, such patterns in living at different altitudes have become more complicated as different ethnic groups live at various levels, and there is greater inter-group mixing. Similarly, the Karen adopted a traditional form of swidden farming operating on a basis of allowing at least seven years before fields were used again, a system which also allowed regrowth of forest. Now, this system has changed as a result of pressure on land use, and changed agricultural practices.

Around 1970 the Royal Thai Government allocated land and land title deeds to those Karen families who could prove their longevity in Thailand and to whom ID cards could be issued. While, for the first time, this gave the Karen within Thailand legality as Thai citizens, this new land classification occurred at the same time as changes in traditional swidden practices. Some impacts were the exhaustion of land fertility, the increased pollution of running and ground water resources, and a variety of other social and economic problems.

Forty years later, there is still a struggle to live in the remote villages. Thousands of Karen people are living several hours from the towns. Some have never been there, the roads being impassable in the rainy season and tracks through the bamboo and teak forests are destroyed with landslides. The Thai government gave most villages a clean water system but often the source was polluted and the subsequent supplies inadequate. Rice remains their staple diet, but sometimes they are restricted in growing dry rice (grown on the side of the mountains) because of the political issues around logging. The rivers often flood their land leaving the paddy rice fields silted up and useless. The heavy rains also bring down trees and rocks on to other fields. The buffalo plough is not strong enough to work these fields and clear the land. Thousands of people still live without clean water and thousands more have no access to a latrine or understand the necessity for hygiene.

The Karen usually live in close-knit communities, with a strong sense of community spirit and high moral and religious values. Karen families are cross-generational, often with grandparents, parents and children living together under the same roof. The average number of children per family is three. Each village is presided over by two headman; an appointed headman, who represents the villagers in external and political affairs; and a "people's" representative headman, who is elected by the people.

The village is run by various committees ensuring a consensus of opinion on all decision making. There is a village committee for education and agricultural issues etc. and the people's headman will be part of that group.

Jenny, a postgraduate from Cambridge university came as a volunteer for two months in 2001 and wrote the following:

It was the women of the village that impressed me the most. I still come back to them as my heroines and hold them up as role models. I was at first fooled into thinking it was the men who command the village – they leave the village first thing and toil the fields all day while the women stay back and tend to the children. But if it is the men who provide for the village it is the women who organise it. These women were strong, practical, astute, whilst warm, kind, caring and open. Nothing fazed them. I can see them now – washing, cleaning, cooking, looking after the children. The more I watched them the more remarkable they were. I have images of women hauling the young ones on their backs up into the jungle, coming to help out at the construction site – and putting us to shame with their machete skills. They were trusting and inquisitive – wanting to interact with us and learn from us. Grandma was the most memorable personality from my stay. She took on the role of matriarch whose age and wisdom were respected by the whole village. There was nothing she did not hear, see or know. She played confidante, handing out her advice to those who asked as well as those who did not. Everyone wanted her approval and she was the only person whose words the children really paid heed to. The headman of the village might have been the head of the village to the outside world but spend anytime inside and it was clear who was running the show.

The last thing I'll never forget about that summer is flying home to the UK on September 11th 2001 as if all that I had learned about the bonds of humanity were being put straight to the test. I took heart then in the lessons I had learned from the Karen. And I still do.

Health is monitored by small health clinics, sometimes up to ten kilometres from a village. Local people are trained to treat malaria and other minor issues. This is important as hospitals can be ninety kilometres from the village but there is no public transport.

Traditionally, they build their stilted houses from teak or bamboo, but due to the restrictions on teak recently, the use of concrete has been introduced. The space underneath the houses is used for animals such as buffalo, pigs, chickens and cows. Although the Government have given them water tanks, the water is not clean enough to use as drinking water, resulting in high levels of typhoid and other water-borne diseases. Often water has to be collected from the rivers and much time is spent collecting and boiling water for drinking. Where they have access to drinking water, their health improves and they have more time in the day to work in the fields and get to schools.

The Karen people have few possessions and usually sleep on mats on the floor. Cooking is over an open fire on earth or the wooden floors of the house. Occasionally, a wooden frame is built to store equipment or to sleep on. There is generally little furniture.

The traditional Karen diet is made up largely of rice, eggs and spices. They eat chicken, pork and fish. There are also fruits such as papaya, banana, mango, lychees, longan, oranges, rambutan and pineapple.

In their beliefs many years ago they were predominantly animist, believing solely in the spirits. As they integrated locally many became Buddhist also believing in the spirits, until the missionaries came in 1826 bringing Christianity. The Catholics often came from the Basque region of France and although there is evidence of French missionaries in Burma up to 400 years ago, they have only been in Thailand around fifty years. Even now I find some Catholic people still need to remember and understand the 'spirit' world and will literally feed the spirits to ensure they are included in their prayers and thoughts. I am reminded by the funeral in the first village I ever went to where someone had died from malaria. They invited me to sit with them around the coffin. Behind the coffin was a large crucifix and on the wooden shelf was a small statue of Our Lady, but on the coffin itself were enamel plates of rice with various spices which were there to feed the spirits.

During my travels over the next few years I discovered spirit houses in the fields and homes of the people and stories where the communication with the spirits were vital in ensuring the 'wholesome' thinking of bringing humanity together with the environment. By then there were villages where they had very strong missionaries directing that all this animist thinking and persuasion of spirits was taboo and against Christian thinking. In my humble opinion, and from what I have learnt and experienced, I find this belief in the spirits reassuring. It is not necessarily tangible, but it brings an understandable mystery to Christianity. My daughter Georgina's experiences as well as those that we experienced after Richard died can be discarded as imagination but the more one understands of the spirit world it has to have a place in our thinking. After all, the Christians talk of the Trinity; God the Father, God the Son and God the Holy Spirit. The Buddhists and Animists just think of the spirit in a different way and every story should be listened to with empathy and understanding as to where the story came from and what it means.

It would seem, from various writings that the 'spirits' can be divided into three groups or divisions: first, those spirits that are thought to dwell apart, to possess human attributes and to control the destiny of men and events; second, the spirits of mortals that for some reason have been condemned to wander about and that have relations, usually evil, with living men; and third, a number of heterogeneous spirits that never were mortal but still can influence men at various times and places. Mostly the spirits will be recognised from the first group although there is evidence of the others too. The thoughts and stories of the influence of the spirit world are too diverse and complex for me to write about here, other than to say they influence birth and death, sickness and health, the water and the land, where people live. Every tree, every lake, every river is supposed to be inhabited by its "k' sa" or divinity. When a man selects the location of his field, he must perform certain ceremonies to win the goodwill of the spirit. The simplest of these is to place an offering of rice and water at the foot of some large tree in the plot chosen before performing specific ceremonies. The chicken too plays an important part with the spirits and often the foot of the chicken is used to decide on the right path to follow.

The Witch Doctor was, and often still is, an important and vital person in the village community. Without a doubt they were able to heal; they had an understanding of local medicines using natural vegetation and spices. However today there are fewer who practise this type of healing, but where they do are revered members of the community.

The climate is very hot and humid. The rainy season starts in May and goes through to October. November, December and January are warm during the day but very cold at night.

The Karen people still weave their own clothes. The women wear long cotton skirts with stripes circulating the body. Their tops are made of two lengths sewn together with long tassels hanging down. They are very colourful and usually made of bright coloured cotton. The patterns woven into the tops are handed down from generation to generation. One top can take up to a month to make but still most village people will take the time to weave. Weaving is done on a strap loom, sitting on the ground pushing their feet against a log and pulling against a piece of buffalo hide round their backs. The loom is attached to the wall of the house and a wooden or bamboo shuttle takes the cotton backwards and forwards through the loom. Sometimes the villagers have the knowledge to use the natural dyes. They are made from using certain roots of trees which are then boiled with rice for several days and depending on the root, so the colour will vary. These are soft colours used on a stronger cotton than the artificial bright colours. In just a few villages it is possible to find the lengths of woven material that were used as headdresses which are now embroidered with seed heads and shells from the rivers and sold to tourists as table runners. These are rare and not made enough for the bigger commercial market, but nevertheless very beautiful.

The music that I had heard when I first came to the villages was very simple and mostly song. There were the excruciating amplifiers in the high schools, but there was no sight of traditional instruments. I put this down to the heat, thinking that string instruments would succumb to the humidity. I forgot about wind instruments, but I certainly did not see any. There was dance, which was rhythmic and swaying and slow and often illustrated a story of life or was connected with hymns. There was one that was repeated in a number of places where the children, dressed as man and woman, were swinging a pretend doll to and fro and the words were telling that man and wife must look after the children together and be good parents. I saw another dance where lengths of bamboo were placed criss-crossing each other on the ground and the dancers had to skip in various sequences over the bamboo, a little akin to some Scottish dances.

Then one day in 2004 I went shopping in Chiang Mai and found a sophisticated shop selling wall hangings. I asked if there were any made by the Karen people. The answer was no, but it prompted more questions. The shop was owned by a Japanese lady called Mieko. She was soon talking to me about Chi. I must meet Chi. His Thai name is Suwichan Phattana Phraiwan. He played the traditional harp and she had just finished making a film about him. So began a good friendship. Chi comes from the Baptist area of north-west Thailand called Wat Chan. The country round there is all pine forests. Chi plays the Karen harp and several other instruments. He told me that his father used to play several traditional instruments and Chi longed to learn to play too. However when Chi tried to play and got the notes wrong, his father would hit him, sometimes across the face and often slap his hand. He was so upset he had to go away and teach himself and only came back to his father when he had learnt. It was rare and still is rare to play the traditional instruments and not always encouraged. One day his father had wanted to play the instruments in the Baptist church, but the Pastor sent him away for such behaviour.

The oldest and most precious of the traditional instruments is the drum. This goes back centuries and it is thought that the place of origin might be the old Cambodian kingdom of the Indo-Chinese peninsula. There are various designs or classes. The Karen drums are characterized by the shape, often in the shape of a dumb bell. They can be huge, measuring some seven feet long and two to three feet in diameter. They are sometimes decorated on the outer edge with frogs. The story goes that if you went to buy a drum you paid according to the number of frogs. The drums make a noise like a gong. Today it is rare to see the drums as the tourists have been intrigued and bought them to take home.

The harp (Karen word is Tehnaku) is a curved instrument often carved in the shape of an animal or bird. They were carved from a tree called Maisaw (Karen word is Kermar). The tree had to be cut as part of the slash and burn programme so the wood was available in the rice fields. While they rested in the rice fields they would carve these instruments, using bamboo to hold the strings in place. The strings were made of thin strips of the banana tree leaf which could then be plucked. The flute would be made from bamboo. There were various shapes of guitar too. I was lucky enough to see these instruments at a concert Chi had organised in the temple in Chiang Mai. Later I was to ask Chi to Bangkok to entertain Thai people at a fundraising function. He has a beautiful voice and was already experienced in broadcasting (see photo).

Chi and I talked at length about his biggest passion. He was so worried that these instruments, the language, the books, the stories and the history would disappear in the future. He was determined to build a cultural centre. He had clearly thought this through. A building for performance space and teaching, a secure place to keep the instruments, a dormitory or hostel where people could come and stay to learn more, a coffee shop or cafe that would bring some income. There would be a place for growing crops so that people could learn about various varieties and uses and sustainability. The important thing was to educate people to these things, to use them, to learn about them. He and a team of friends were working on a business plan. I could only help by listening and observing when I felt it needed more focus. The whole concept must be good. He is right. His enthusiasm was infectious. As a very committed Christian he knows that when the time is right God will provide, but he is impatient with enthusiasm. I have every confidence that he will succeed and I hope I am around long enough to see it.

Chapter Ten

Li Shau Wai and the
Story of the Golden Book

Before the American Baptist missionaries came to bring Christianity in 1826, there was no alphabet in the Karen language. There was a 'kind' of language but it was a bit 'scratch'. Story has it that in 1880 Father Jo went to Burma to collect the new alphabet from the Baptists and bring it back to Thailand. This was the Roman script that the missionaries had brought with them. Up to then it had been just a spoken language. The sad thing is that today's Karen people don't learn to read or write Karen. They speak it in their families, but they have to learn Thai at school. Then they also have to learn English. When they go back to the families they only speak it. Stories and history are passed down by word of mouth. Although some Baptists and academics have documented the written language, the younger generation today will lose sight of it. They often sat in the evening around the fire and told stories but life has changed and life is busy. They no longer sit in the evenings, telling stories as they did. Chi is right to be worried.

The following story is a rather delightful folk story about how **Li Shau Wai** (pronounced Lee Chor Weh) the Scratch Chicken Script, as it was known, came to the Karen people. It was told to me by several different people. Many of the older generation know this story but it has not often been passed down to the younger people simply because families do not gather in the evenings for bedtime stories anymore.

The story of the Golden Book – The root of the Karen language

God gave the Karen people a gold book. God gave to the English a silver book. But to the other people he gave nothing.

The English wanted to know what was in the gold book so they asked to borrow it. They copied the book. The Karen people did not have time to read the gold book as they were busy working in the rice fields. When the English people came to return the book, the Karen people asked them to put it on the fence and they would collect it at the end of the day. But the Karen people forgot and left the book on the fence. A month goes by and the rice has now become yellow. The wild chickens are coming to eat the rice and as they flew into the rice field, they knocked the gold book off the fence. It fell on to the ground amongst the yellow rice. The chickens were scratching around for the rice, some of which was on the gold book. The gold book became very scratched.

When the others came along they said: "What is this?" The Karen people said this is our gold book that God gave us. The others asked if they could borrow it. But they only gave back half the book. So the Karen people said to God: "Please give us another book because the one you gave us has gone." But God said, "No. You should have looked after it and now you must wait for another day. Your cousins, the English people will bring you another one." But the English people did not, and they are still waiting.

Some say that this is the beginning of the 'scratch' alphabet. Some people even today speak a strange language which is thought to be illustrated by the Scratch Chicken story.

Postscript: The Karen animists were angry with the chickens for scratching the book. Today they will kill the chicken and use bones for black magic and to analyze problems.

Chapter Eleven

Wat Prabhat Huay Tom – The Village of Ghosts and the Footprints of Khru Ba

The village where the silver is made

The name is explained like this: Wat means 'temple'. Prabhat means 'footprint of Buddha', Huay means 'small river' or 'stream'. Tom means 'boil'.

Wat Prabhat Huay Tom is situated 150 kilometres south of Chiang Mai in the district of Lamphun. Taking the road due south of Hod on Route 108 you pass through the small town of Li and find the main entrance to the whole village on your right. The straight road ahead of you takes you past small, poor Karen stilted houses and more roads at right angles to other parts of the village. At the end of the first road is a large white temple, obviously still under construction. I came here a few years ago when Salahae brought me to see how the silver jewellery was made. I knew that this was the only village in the whole of Thailand where the silver is made, but I had no idea why and I had no idea about the history of this village. It was, even then, the largest number of Karen people living in one village and today has a population of 15,000 people.

All around is flat country with no mountains in sight. Uninteresting, no rice fields, no obvious reason why the Karen people would live here. I had first come to see the silver because we wanted to sell it in the UK not just to raise extra funds but also to raise the profile of the skills of the Karen people.

The silver industry is fascinating. The Karen people have only been in this village for around forty years. With no rice growing (because there was no water), they found they were encouraged by the King through the Royal Projects to work with silver. They began to melt down silver rupees and tap silver into various forms of jewellery. Now they buy silver from Chiang Mai by weight, sometimes in very small balls. Turning a log of wood on its end, they place the silver on the top and melt it down with a hand held blow lamp using a foot pump. Then each member of the family will tap tap tap the melted piece into different shapes, sometimes flattening it to weave into bangles, sometimes tapping it into small balls for necklaces or rings. Even the clasps are made by melting each piece and then moulding and gluing them all together. All the tools are made in the village. It is a huge industry, very dependent on the world price of silver and the world economy. It is so ethnically made that it is very appealing in today's market. Not only is it sold as necklaces, bracelets and earrings in the shops and bazaars of Chiang Mai and Bangkok but little pieces are used to link with precious stones by jewellery designers all over the world.

On that early visit, I had visited the temples, of which there were five. The first I saw was a plain white building still under construction. Inside around forty paintings hung high on the wall above the high windows. Each painting was, I was told, sketched out by the visionary monk before he died and now was being copied, as he had directed, onto these amazing pictures. They were not complete. I also visited the huge gold and highly decorated temple, known as Wat Prabhat Huay Tom. Here I saw the embalmed body of the monk in a glass coffin sitting high on a plinth. He was under a huge, domed, artificial tree. The base was surrounded by a very large number of small buddhas. Each and every Buddha had a little food and water set in front of them as is traditional Buddhist custom. All around the edge of the building were a very large quantity of carved busts of monks which I understood to have been made by this visionary monk to remember those he had worked with. On the walls, but I could barely see them for the quantity of sculpted busts, were large paintings, some of them quite horrifically illustrating what happens to those who sin.

Now in 2009 I was coming again to learn more about the history. I had brought Nootsabar, our Karen assistant, with me to translate and another Thai friend called Kru Toy, the wife of our very good friend, the head teacher Attaset in Mae Hong Son. We made straight for the house of Adoon. I had met Adoon on my first visit with Salahae and he was now ready to help us with any kind of information. Adoon had lived in the village for thirty years and had been involved in working the silver and developing the business, had been appointed headman of the village and was now a politician representing his people.

The story of Wat Prabhat Huay Tom has now been well documented in Thai and a book is available. But I don't speak Thai, so I was here to learn from Adoon.

He told us that 100 years ago there had been a city on the site called Lap Lae (meaning 'mystic place'). It had been lived in by Thai people, but there had been a lot of fighting and problems. The Thai people found it difficult to live there and had given up. Now there were so many ghosts it was quite impossible for Thai people as they were frightened of ghosts. There was no water and no possibility of growing crops. The Lawa people lived on these plains at the time and built low houses as there was no water and no worries about flooding. Some still live in this area. Then came the famous Karen visionary monk whose name was Khru Ba Chaiwongsa. He had come to the village at the age of fifty having previously been at Doi Suthep near Chiang Mai.

The story goes that in October 1971 he called the people of Mae Hong Son and Lamphun and Chiang Mai and told them to come and see the new village. He said they must not kill animals but it was important they came. He needed them to help him build a temple. There was no water so they were told they had to dig four large holes. They then had to pray for seven days and seven nights and they found a spring and water came and the lakes are full of water today. Khru Ba said this is the centre of Thailand for the Karen people and he called more Karen to ask for help from the King's Royal projects. The Thai people could not help because they are afraid of ghosts.

I asked Adoon if he saw ghosts sometimes. "Oh yes," he said. "There is a beautiful lady in the Pho tree. She does not stay long, but I see her."

So for eight years after the people came to the village there was no work. No water, no rice to be grown and nothing else.

Now, on this visit to the village I was visiting the big white temple again. This time all the paintings were complete. They told the story of Khru Ba's life and the development of the village. The first painting showed the young boy with his parents. Then he was collecting vegetables from the forest as there was nothing else to eat. Soon after he became a young monk (many children in Thailand become monks for a short time). He did his lessons and learnt about Buddha and was soon playing with the other children and teaching them good things. He talked to the Karen from the Tak province and told them to wear Karen clothes and protect their culture.

Above each of the main doors of this temple is a tripdtych depicting the fierce dragon who is there to frighten the ghosts.

The paintings continued. So the people live in the forests eating bananas and oranges and good fruit but they come from Tak province to be with Khru Ba. He starts to build a Karen house for them and they love him very much. So they carry him around on their shoulders. Then another monks arrives and asks to stay with Khru Ba. He has come to record information and data. From then on other monks come. Khru Ba and his new monk collect more Karen people but they can only stay if they refuse to kill animals. Now he has built the little Karen stilted houses, he must build a road. Then the pictures show a team of Karen digging a big hole for the lake of which there will ultimately be four. Now they must build the temple. First they have to decide where it is to be built and they must wait for certain guidance about this. They have to choose a certain day to start, depending on the spirit. So the people start to build the road, but this means cutting the trees down. The temple is nearly finished but the monks must now take a black bowl and spray it with good water to get rid of any bad spirits. Soon after the temple is finished, the tourists come. This is a lovely picture of a modern car arriving with people in western dress, in contrast to the other paintings of people in Karen clothing.

Soon after Khru Ba has to go and see the people of Om Koi but it is far, so there is a rather incongruous picture of the helicopter flying high over the mountains and landing amongst the Karen people of Om Koi. With the village nearly complete it is time to paint a map of the village. Khru Ba invites the King to visit. Next he uses cotton to place a bracelet round the wrist of the King to bring him good health. (Picture as illustrated.) And the final picture shows all the Karen people with Khru Ba praying together in thanksgiving.

Thinking how amazing this is, I am not really prepared for what I see next. Adoon took us to the main temple of Wat Prabhat Huay Tom. The last time I had seen this, it had been very overcrowded and difficult to understand the story. Now standing before us was a new building; utterly spectacular in its height, in its proportions, in its decorations and statues. There were very few people about. There is a small shop just inside the gates of the complex and an ice cream man with his bike. To the right there are long buildings where the monks eat and do lessons. We left our shoes at the foot of the stairs to this spectacular building and went inside. It was breathtaking. All walls were painted white. No paintings anywhere, but in front of us was a huge beautiful gold Buddha. Very high. The Buddha was looking down on a glass case in which lay the gold, embalmed body of Khru Ba, still with his woolly hat on his head. This glass case was so high on a plinth of marble, that we could hardly see him.

Then we went to the room behind where we found the painted wall pictures that I had discovered before. Now they were free from the clutter of sculpted monks and I could see them more clearly. Whereas the paintings in the first temple had depicted the history of Khru Ba and the development of Wat Prabhat Huay Tom, these large paintings told of the moral issues and the dangers of sin. There were five commandments that must be obeyed.

1. No cheating or fornication
2. No killing
3. No lying
4. No alcohol
5. No gambling

The pictures depicted the terrible things that would happen to you if you broke these rules. You would certainly be thrown naked into a big cauldron of boiling water and fire. All around this large room the paintings continued to show graphic pictures of fornication, drunkenness and other bad things. The paintings taught the importance of praying for forgiveness; of giving food and offerings to the poor and of giving flowers and showing love. Animals and humans must co-exist. The monk will go to learn from God in heaven and Buddha will teach the monk to be a leader. The leader will then tell the Gods when you do good things and help the poor people and you will get good things for yourself. So long as everyone keeps the five rules then the world will be happy. Good harvests will come in the future.

I came away slightly in awe of the large numbers of very large paintings. Adoon then invited us to walk round the outside of the temple and there on the long outside walls were MORE paintings. I thought by now that I knew the whole story and was not really concentrating. However after a few minutes my attention was caught by the words Lawa hilltribe. The Lawa hilltribe had heard about Khru Ba and came to ask him for some hair from his head; but the monk said they had nowhere to keep it. He said that he would make a footprint for them in stone. So they went to find a large stone and carried it to the monk. Then they wet it and the monk stood on the stone and made his footprints. This is the picture of the people and the big stone with the footprints, that gave me the name for this book (see front cover).

Then we were taken to another building where we were shown two huge footprint shaped spaces set onto a large square marbled plinth. It was like a tomb in itself and obviously revered. A long length of bamboo was arranged so that on occasions water can be channelled into the footprint spaces. The actual stone marked with the real footprints is preserved under the footprint baths that we could see.

As we left we were taken to the side of the temple to see the well where the initial water had been found by Khru Ba with his 'staff'. Outside the main temple is a very large tree, the Pho Tree, now surrounded by spirit houses and places to pray. This was the place where Khru Ba sat for hours in prayer.

Today the temples form part of a monastery with 100 monks living there, some of them being children as young as six. So there is a teaching place, accommodation and other places for prayer and meditation. To one side of the big temples is an octagonal building – another temple but inside this one it is made of glass and prisms. In the centre of this temple is a Buddha hanging from the roof space and eight modern people, rather strangely dressed in shorts and shirts, looking in from above. This is 'for the people', I was told.

And all of this is set in this large sprawling village on flat land where every family is involved in the making of silver which is now sold all over the world.

This village and its story confirmed to me all that I have learnt about the Karen people and their history. Nowhere else in the whole of Thailand is so much information available about the Karen people – and yet so few people ever make the journey to see it.

Appendices

Projects

Our aim was to help the Karen people to help themselves to build a better future and the best way to do this was to focus on three things;

1. Improve health by installing clean water systems, improving sanitation and the provision of blankets and mosquito nets.
2. Improve access to education through the provision of transport and food, building and improving dormitories, sponsorship of students to college and university.
3. Improve opportunities for generating income through irrigation systems and regenerating land. Also establishing outlets for natural crafts.

1. Improving health

Installation of clean water systems and latrines

When we talk about installing clean water systems, many people imagine that we are installing drilled wells. It has been tried many times but Salahae soon realized that it was not possible to drill deep enough to produce water for twelve months of the year on an ongoing basis. In any case, generators would be needed to install the drills. The Karen people could also not afford to buy new pumps when they broke. The important thing was to give the Karen people clean potable water that would run for twelve months of the year for the next twenty years. To do this it is necessary to find a water source that comes from a natural spring. Only the local Karen people would be likely to know where there was such a natural spring. It had to be above the levels of pollution, above where the animals were grazing, above where there were likely to be chemicals on the land. Sometimes this natural spring is several kilometres from the village. It has to be high. The source then has to be dammed. Sand and gravel have to be brought up from the river bed some distance below. Salahae will order the appropriate quantity of pipes to be delivered to the village. This can be difficult because in the rainy season the roads are very bad. Once the equipment has arrived the pipes, concrete and cement have to be carried the several kilometres up the mountain to the source which is then dammed. A filter tank is built close to the source and the water will pass through charcoal, sand and gravel before travelling through the pipes that have been dug into shallow trenches, all the way down the mountain. Sometimes the terrain is along the side of a steep mountain, sometimes alongside the river and up the other side. The distance can be anything from one to twelve kilometres. It is gravity fed and it is important the pressure is right. Once the water reaches the village, large 10,000 litre tanks must be built. Because the land is subject to landslides the ground for these tanks must be firm. A base of stone is made. Wires are taken upwards to reinforce the tanks. Moulds are used into which the concrete is poured and the tanks are sealed at the top. A small square area is left for the water to pass through a piece of gauze into the tank. The water will then come from the bottom of the tank and is taken in more shallow trenches, down the village street to where standpipes will be built for taps. We aim to put one tap for every three houses.

The installation of these water systems requires all the village people to agree that it is needed and to help with the installation. Salahae and his staff will do a full survey and evaluation of the village – how many children, how many female/adult, how far to the nearest school, what crops do they grow, how many pipes of what size are required, plus a whole lot more information which is then sent to the UK office for approval. Once the system is complete, they will be instructed on how to maintain the system. We also build small huts housing a squat latrine and an extra tap that can be used for showering. They are given basic lessons in hygiene and a supply of soap.

The Karen people are full of excitement. Never before have they have been able to drink water from a tap. Never before have they had so much time to do other jobs in the village. Their health will improve dramatically. The local government are more likely to give them electricity. They suddenly have hope. They kill a pig and have a party, sing songs and drink moonshine whisky.

Health records will be noted in the initial survey and then checked later. In principle there is a ninety per cent reduction in typhoid once they have clean water. Malaria is also reduced although this is not a waterborne disease. Stomach problems are also reduced, but difficult to monitor.

2. Improving access to education

Thousands of children still do not have access to education because they live too far away from a secondary school and do not have any money for transport, accommodation or food. KHT helps with all these projects. For those who have been lucky enough to get to school, there is the chance of sponsorship to university following which many of them come back to be near their families and work in their local area.

All our volunteers make a difference to the lives of the Karen people, but those who get involved in teaching give them a confidence that enables them to take their place more easily alongside the Thai students. There has been one volunteer to whom we owe a particular debt of gratitude. At the age of seventy-two, Jean Collinson went out to Thailand to study the issues at primary level in the area of Khun Yuam. A life long girl guide and a senior primary school lecturer, she had all the relevant experience and certainly the determination to make a real difference. She lived with the Karen people in their primitive village and caught the bus with the children to school. She made wonderful friends with teachers at all levels and gained their confidence, developing methods of teaching that could be understood and were fun. Today most of the children she taught over a period of six years, now have a place at secondary school and many are going on to university. Her influence set a precedence that many volunteers have benefited from since. Since she married for the first time she has now retired from her visits to Thailand but continues to help me in the office in York.

The construction and repairs to dormitories has been another key project.

Building the dormitory at Huay Kai Pa
On my second visit to Thailand, in 1999, I went again to the village of Ban Huay Kai Pa (Wild Chicken Village). The village was forty minutes north-west of the small town of Mae La Noi which is where the nearest hospital and high school are situated. The population was around 400 people. A primary school was in the village and children old enough to go to secondary school had to stay in a dormitory in Mae La Noi, only coming back at weekends or sometimes staying away for several months. There were never enough places at the dormitory and in any case, they had to pay 100thb (£1.50) a month for food and many families could not afford this.

The key man in the village was known as Boonmuang and I got to know him, his wife and most of their children quite well. I sometimes stayed in their house. The house was made of teak but as the years went by and the Government got more concerned about the environment, teak became expensive and the lower levels of the house were filled in with concrete. Volunteers from all over the world had come to spend several months in his house, to help with teaching at the local primary school and sometimes to help install water systems. They found wonderful hospitality, friendship and laughter; a house overflowing with people from the surrounding area, children and friends. Boonmuang was the headman at the time and much respected. A great character, covered in tattoos and a lifetime of experience. He drove the most amazing truck that looked as if it had seen World War II but often the only way to get to remote villages was by driving along the river beds, over the rocks and up the mountain tracks. So the condition of the vehicle was not surprising.

On this particular visit, Boonmuang took me to see the dormitory which was situated just next door to the primary school at the far end of the village. The dormitory consisted of two buildings beside each other, both constructed of bamboo. The roofs were made of large teak leaves sewn onto bamboo rods. They were very weak buildings (see photo).

The floors were full of big gaps, the walls did not meet the roof at the ends. Each building had just one room and housed twenty-five children. The children barely had a change of clothes, but there was certainly nowhere to store them. There were no latrines. The children had to go across the road to the primary school or use the nearby forest. There was no electricity. The cold in the winter months and the mosquitos in the long hot rainy season made life very difficult, but then the children knew nothing else. Boonmuang told me that there was no money to pay for food. The caretaker received no wages. He told me the buildings were in a bad state and would not last another year. Then he said: "Wouldn't it be wonderful if you could find the money for us and there could be a KHT dormitory in Huay Kai Pa?" I was slightly taken aback and started to worry. These children needed a lot of help, but then so did many people in virtually every village I visited. To build a dormitory would cost a lot of money and I had no idea where I would find enough money to build a stronger building, nor did I know what kind of building to build, or where. How much would it cost to run and who would run it? I had no idea who owned land in the village or what the local issues would be. I ruled out being able to help and returned to the UK.

Two weeks after getting home, I had a letter from an ex-volunteer called Abigail. She had not been in touch for ages. In fact I was about to take her off our mailing list because it was costing money to send out ongoing newsletters, so unless people responded I did not know if they were interested. Then suddenly this letter came. She had run in the London marathon and raised £2,000 and was writing now to ask if there was anything we could spend it on. As Abigail had lived in Huay Kai Pa for five months and taught in the primary school, the obvious purpose for this money was to rebuild the dormitory. I was excited and very grateful to Abigail. I rang Salahae. He rang Boonmuang. News travelled fast and I was soon told that there was a piece of land, still in the village, which we could rent. The building would have to be constructed quickly to ensure there were facilities for the fifty children in time for the new school year the following May. Huge teak posts were brought in, but the walls would still be made of bamboo. Bamboo must be cut at specific times of year (and maturity) to prevent it getting eaten by weevils but we did not have time to wait. Even if the building lasted five years, it would be worth it. We brought in running water and electricity. There was a kitchen space with a fridge. Ex-volunteers were told of this project and we soon raised enough money to feed the children and pay the caretaker. People in Bangkok paid for blankets and mosquito nets.

The trouble was that we did not own the land. This meant that the dormitory was at risk if the landowner wanted the land back. This is exactly what began to happen. Three years after building, we had to think again while we persuaded him to allow us time to search elsewhere. Talks began again with the village people as to what to do next. All Karen villages have a village committee with an education sub committee. In Huay Kai Pa, there were about three representatives who came to talk to me. They had an idea. There was a piece of land on the outskirts of the village in a field by the river. It was apparently owned by the village committee, so it would not be a problem to get them to agree for a permanent dormitory to be built on this land. All that was needed was for five people to meet on the site. Each person would point to a different corner of the site and altogether they would just raise their thumbs to the sky showing agreement. This could be recorded in writing. They were quite serious about this. So at 7.00am I went to meet the committee with Boonmuang. Each person (one was a child) pointed to the corner of the site and everyone raised their thumbs. Great! We now had confirmation. Now I had to contact the lawyer in Bangkok and try and explain that the village committee were happy for the dormitory to go ahead. He was amused, to say the least, but this was hardly the right way to proceed.

Another year went by and the search for land continued. Then a small teak plantation on the side of the road to Huay Ku Pa and Huay Kong Paw became available. Seven rais of land could be bought for £5,000. The teak alone had a value, although the trees were still thin but in time would be valuable. We suddenly had a big project ahead. We would have to buy this land through the Foundation for the Karen Hilltribes in Thailand. We would need to get deeds drawn up by lawyers in Bangkok who would need to have all documents translated from Karen into Thai and then into English. We would need to draw up plans for the actual building and then find funding. We were advised that we should use Thai architects but the difficulties of getting Thai architects to manage a project so far from Chiang Mai and deep in the forests, where Karen people understood their local suppliers much better than those from the city was difficult. I had to go through the process to satisfy those funders that we had explored all avenues and got the best prices.

In the end I discovered Mr Damrong, a local Karen construction engineer who had built several local Catholic churches and dormitories and was much respected. Certainly his drawings were not as sophisticated as those from the bigger companies, but I understood and was assured of the quality. His prices were by far the cheapest and he could construct it quickly, using local labour. We were immensely fortunate to find a funder who sponsored the building of the dormitory for £30,000 and the running costs for the first twelve months. It now houses eighty children who are looked after by two carers and a manager. Some of the children live anything from ten to 100kms away and can only go home every six months. None of them have any money to cover the running costs. Families in these very remote mountain areas are still very poor. The villages are often only sixty per cent self sufficient in rice with no money to buy the rest. The dormitory is monitored by Salahae with accounts being sent back to the UK monthly. It is such a success story that after the first year, the dormitory was funded by the Conrad Hotel in Bangkok through their guests. Since then we have a wonderful philanthropic supporter who has funded it for five years. Let us hope we can keep this up.

3. Improving Income Generation:
Karen people grow coffee, fruit, garlic, mushrooms, soya and rice. They have buffalo, cows, pigs and chickens. Rice is their staple diet and yet some villages are still only forty per cent or at most sixty per cent self sufficient in rice. We have tried to find a solution that will help them to help themselves through trading some of these products but it is fraught with difficulties. Middlemen need to be educated people, language is a barrier. The Karen villages are too far from the big towns and the cost of travel is too great. They have to compete with the Hmong people who are natural traders and undercut them. The village people are let down by the big traders who might promise to buy crops such as coffee and then change their minds.

With the devastating effects of floods and landslides, when land goes out of production and crops cannot grow, we have found that the most effective and helpful project is to clear the debris and put the land back into production. This gives them control of their own lives and the ability to generate their own income. The small buffalo plough is inadequate for this job. Thanks to a generous donor we have a large New Holland tractor that is much in demand. We employ a Karen driver who spends two weeks in a village clearing fields and valleys of debris and deeply ploughing the land. How wonderful it is to see such valleys lush with the green of young good quality rice and to meet the local people who are so, so pleased to be able to work in the fields again, generating their own income and taking control of their own lives.

Irrigation projects are invaluable in crop production Water needs to be channeled from the river to the fields using dams or canals. However they are often weak (due to lack of funds) and get easily damaged in the heavy rains. Many acres of land are out of production through lack of water. KHT has funded stronger irrigation systems, both for dams across the rivers as well as the canals which take the water along the side of the of the river and into fields This is a very important project in income generation and putting the controls back in the hands of the Karen people (see picture).

The traditional weaving skills go back centuries and the Karen people still weave their own clothes and bags. Sometimes the Karen use natural dyes that are made by boiling certain roots of trees with rice for many hours to get certain colours. At other times very bright artificial dyes are used. KHT buys some of the bags for sale in the UK and online which not only provides a small outlet for the Karen people but also raises the profile of their skills around the world. Although the silver jewellery is only made in Wat Prabhat Huay Tom it is sold in the shops in Chiang Mai and Bangkok. KHT buys the silver jewellery to sell in the UK and on line. This also raises the profile and the skills of the Karen people and helps to keep the traditional skills alive.

Appendix Two

Karen Lessons in Hospitality: A Personal Story from Una, an Ex-Volunteer

After over sixteen hours of flying in three air planes, an eight hour bumpy bus ride, a hair-raising one hour ride in the back of a jeep, a quick jaunt in a heavily-laden motorbike across the wooden bridge slung across a gorge and finally I nervously entered the community that would be my home for the next two months. Ban Huay Kai Pa Pa – a beautiful hilltribe village of ninety bamboo huts on teak stilts set in the mountainous jungles of Northern Thailand. Along with my twin sister, I volunteered for the Karen Hilltribes Trust as an English teacher the summer after my first year of medical school. I had entered a place both completely physically and culturally remote from any previous life experience. As I helped pound rice with the misty monsoon mountains emerging in the dawn with my hilltribe grandmother weaving and laughing beside me, I could not have been further from my first year at university. Soon it was just normal to help skin pigs freshly killed, to go hunting with the village chief in the jungle, and run with the children to collect bananas and bamboo shoots as a tasty treat.

During my two month stay with the Karen, I experienced the true meaning of hospitality. The village embraced the two clumsy Westerners and shared their rice, bananas, babies and laughter with us. On leaving, I felt ridiculous with my 65-litre rucksack hoisted on my back. Why do I think I need so much material goods to survive when the Karen have only family, a sense of humour, and their resilience to live off. Although I may not miss the lizards in the squat toilets, the chopping of wood that commenced after we had been offered a cup of Thai tea, or the cockerels at 6am – more than the stunning scenery will stay with me as memories and lessons of a lifetime.

As I was flying home in a Thai Airways jumbo jet, I had views of landscapes incorporating what must be Burma, Bangladesh, the Himalayas and Eastern Europe. It struck me that all the way down there, sprawled over the Earth are thousands, millions of little villages, all celebrating their own unique cultures and enjoying life through the sharing of laughter, in the same way as the inspirational people I met in Ban Huay Kai Pa Pa.

A very Karen Wedding

Nootsabar invited us to one of her cousin's wedding that was taking place in two days time in a village about twenty miles south of where we were staying. We jumped at the chance, and so with very vague instructions of getting off the Southbound bus when we saw a big school to our left, off we set at 7.00am to the bus stop, through the misty mountains, squashed on the back of our host father's motorbike, and on to Ban Nong Haeng.

Nootsabar had said that we would meet her there, yet nobody even seemed to recognise her name on our enquiries. We later realised we had made a school-boy error in using her Thai name, instead of her Karen Name – "amosa-heigh" (meaning "spicy"). After attracting a lot of attention, the headmaster of the school pointed us in the direction of the natural hot springs, assuming that was what we were looking for. We were more than happy to pass some time there, but before we arrived, a very pretty Karen Girl called tee-gay ("beautiful water") zoomed up to us on a scooter, motioning to us to jump on the back of her motorbike. With the blind-faith that comes with Karen-living, we were immediately taken under the wing of all the village women, who were preparing vast amounts of food for the wedding the next day. The day was happily spent perched on logs peeling garlic and chopping green beans, with the whole village in party atmosphere. Music was playing and various offspring arrived back from the bigger towns where they went to school, to join in the party.

Nootsabar finally arrived, and with her translation, the village women asked us with respectful curiosity what our home was like, and one woman jokingly said she would build me a bamboo hut to live in if I married her son! Later in the afternoon, we ate rice with the young adults, who later took us up to the hot springs to boil some eggs and eat avocado fresh from the tree. The bride-to-be happily dressed us in beautiful Karen woven-dresses and bead necklaces. This was to be the last day that she would wear her long white dress, as from tomorrow her attire would be in the colourful skirt and top, the symbol of a married woman. We were excitedly given a tour of the village by the proud children, while the men got to work killing and skinning a cow. The party atmosphere that evening was lovely to be a part of; moonshine, laughter and beer were all in full flow. The young couple were calmly chatting to their many relatives and friends that had descended into the village for the celebrations. How the event was communicated is anyone's guess, but the guests would soon disappear back to their own tribes as suddenly as they had appeared.

The wedding morning started early, with the ceremony taking place in the village Church. The Catholic priest was the well-spoken and wise Father Dominic, who immediately praised his "good friend Penelope" and the work she does in Thailand. He rotates around many hilltribe villages in the area, and so whilst Mass is said every week in the village, there may only be a priest present once a month. As a practising Catholic in the UK, I could recognize the structure and format of the Mass, although our Western slow hymns are replaced with typical Karen singing, where the emphasis is on volume rather than key. I do not know enough about how Catholicism came to be instilled in so many Karen villages, yet I observed that the Karen did not seem to be culturally tuned into it, and no wonder with "Farang" looking statues of the Virgin Mary and Jesus. Much more emphasis is put on their Karen culture and traditions, with their Catholic religion taking a definite side-line. Many people floated in and out during the casual ceremony, although everyone was wearing their best Karen attire. The service itself was over by 8am, and so the wedding breakfast was in full flow soon after. The bigger the occasion, the spicier the food, and so us two foreigners had to gulp many a glass of water during that meal.

To finish off the event, a procession was made through the village from the bride's old house to her new home. Here, it is custom of each guest to tie a piece of string around the wrists of the new couple, and wedding gifts of as much money as each family could afford was placed in a discreet envelope by their side.

I felt so privileged to be a part of the whole wedding celebrations, and made a mental note to welcome strangers wherever I am – even if it is on my wedding day!

Una Finnegan – July and August 2007

Appendix Three

Karen Fables

1. The Hare and the King

Once upon a time, there was a king who was so proud that he was unbearable to all of his subjects. One day, a hare, having heard of this king, went to rebuke him to try to bring him to his senses.

The hare marched into the court of the king and called out, "Hey, you fellow, who do you think you are that you mistreat and look down on your subjects so severely?"

The king answered, "I am the king." To that the hare replied, "Well, I am only a jungle beast, and don't know what 'king' means." "A king is one who has nothing above him," was the reply.

"Well I declare! Is there nothing above you?" questioned the hare. "Nothing," answered the king.

"Well, I never saw a man with nothing above him before, so I want to take a good look at you."

"Look your fill," the king replied. The hare stared at the king for hours, till an urgent call of nature led the king to stir. The hare called out, "Hey, you king, where are you going to?" The king, abashed, sat down again, and went on with his business. This was repeated several times, till the king could hold out no longer, and blurted out, "If you must know, I am going." "Ah! you are no king," shouted the hare, "Your own bowels are your master. They demand food, and you are powerless to resist; they send you on private errands, which you are compelled to do." The king stood silent as the hare continued, "In fact, you are powerless against death, sickness, and old age like all your subjects. No one is above them." The king, pondering on all of this asked the hare, "If I am not the king, then who is the king?" The hare replied, "There is only one king and he is God. We are all his subjects and there is nothing above him."

The king finally understood. Humbled by this new realization, from that day on the King began to rule his subjects with fairness and respect. Thanks to the hare.

2. The Two Sisters in the Rice Fields

Two beautiful sisters went to work in the rice fields. It was very hard work. The older sister said they needed a man to help them with such hard work. A very handsome man came and asked the girls what they were doing. They said: "We are working hard in the rice fields, but it is too much and we need a man to help us." The older sister said, "If a handsome man comes to help us I will marry him."

The handsome man was really a lion who was hungry and wanted to eat the beautiful girls. So he said to the girls that they must cover their eyes for a while and when they uncovered their eyes they would be able to see how much work he had done. So the older sister covered her eyes with a blindfold tied behind her head, but the younger sister just covered her eyes with her hands so that she could peep between her fingers.

While the sisters had covered their eyes the handsome man changed into a lion and then did all the work that was needed in the fields. The older sister then looked and congratulated him, but the younger sister had seen that he was really a lion and she became frightened that he would eat them both up. The older sister followed the lion to the house and the younger sister said, "Be careful. He is going to eat you up."

Then the younger sister sent for the eagle to carry them away. The eagle took them to a rubber tree. The lion decided that if he bit the trunk the tree would fall and he could get the sisters, but the tree was too tough. So he went to get an axe to cut the tree down. So the eagle flew away with the sisters to a banana tree which has very large leaves. From here they could escape and they ran back to the house and hid. But the lion came to the house. "Now I will eat you up, because you have escaped." "No," said the sister. "Don't eat me. I have come home to boil the whisky and prepare the food for our wedding." So the lion came back with five more lions. Although they were dressed as handsome men, their tails could be seen hanging down under their coats. The chickens saw these tails hanging down and sang a song. Chuck, chuck, chuck – cock-a-doodle doo. This song was meant to warn the sisters but they did not understand what the chickens were trying to say. The wedding celebrations began and the village people gave lots of whisky to the lions and got them very drunk. The people killed the big lion, but the mother put her daughter in a box to save her from the five lions. They were so drunk that they did not notice when the tails of the five lions were cut off. At the same time they cut off the head of the big lion and it rolled away and bit a big hole in the wooden box which was hiding the daughter. The head of the lion bit so hard that it bit right through the wood and bit the toe of the daughter and she bled to death.

Moral of the story? Don't always trust everyone. Watch what is going on behind your back.

Grandma's Gin and Lizard Curry

By David Thompson following a visit to the Karen people near Khun Yuam

As printed in the Financial Times (17 Sept. 05)

"I was met by Salahae who took me to his parents-in-law's home where we stayed the night. We were greeted warmly and welcomed with some local rice moonshine. Sipping gingerly, we prepared a rustic dinner in a truly rustic kitchen. As the liquor hit home – they were very generous hosts – we chatted about their life and their food while we picked herbs and dinner was prepared. As my sips became slurps, I thought it would be an excellent idea to show them some of our moonshine, so I pulled out a bottle of English gin. They knocked this back – neat. Grandma became a bit of a gin fiend as she polished off more than her fair share. Next came the Campari, which they preferred as the bitterness reminded them of strong herbal medicine. They took their medication straight. We had quite a late dinner and a mostly excellent one as we sat down on the hard wooden floor and ate from a shared platter of boiled ruddy coloured rice, grown by the family. I ate lightly even though the food was delicious: it was just that the floor was so uncomfortable that it was difficult to eat. It was much easier to talk. The Karen are a very open people and Salahae talked about the difficulties that this community faced. The very remoteness which makes the communities so untouched, means they are isolated during the long rainy season from May to October. This also means that the area's clean water supply and electricity supply is erratic. They were extremely grateful for the support of the Karen Hilltribes Trust in this respect.

"Sleep came easily that night, even though the drone of the insects was extremely loud (it was the rainy season and the crickets were noisy) and I recall having the most fantastic dreams. The next morning we awoke quite early with a wee headache. But this did not matter as we were going on a picnic. Although the small town of Khun Yuam is itself remote, we drove for several harrowing hours along winding, precipitous and muddy roads into the mountainous hinterland. Once we finally reached the ramshackle village that was our destination, we stopped to chat and have a truly welcome cup of green, slightly bitter tea. The rough collection of wooden and stilted houses was clustered along dirt alley ways. We trekked uphill through the jungle and as I struggled and stumbled through the jungle, the agile Karen veered off the track to collect lunch. As I trudged up the hill they pointed out various herbs that can used in place of salt, herbs to quell a stomach ache and even one to quench thirst. Banana blossoms and stalks, sprightly wild bitter herbs and ferns, aubergines of all sorts and glorious wild figs were all collected for the pot.

"As the others started to prepare the meal, one of the lads brought out his stock of rice wine and started to pour some bamboo shooters. The night before came rushing back as I sipped it gingerly once again, although this time it was like swallowing bamboo slivers.

"They brought more of their own rice and some dried fish but everything else was gathered en route. The purplish rice was briskly washed before being poured into the long stalks of bamboo and covered with plenty of water and the end stopped with a clump of rolled banana leaves. Every few minutes the bamboo was turned to ensure the grains cooked evenly. This is an ancient method of cooking and stalks of charred bamboo can be seen in rural markets of the north. Once cooked, the rice looked unpromising as it was spooned on to banana leaves. As it cooled it developed a deeply pleasing slightly bitter nuttiness. Eaten by itself the rice was good but when eaten with the other dishes it became ambrosial. I began to understand why this rice is so venerated.

"With it we had a nutty vegetable soup, geng rorn, with shredded banana blossoms, stalks from the banana tree, galangal and toasted soy beans. And a very unusual cold soup, geng yen, made by steeping dried mustard greens, shallots, chillies and coriander in water. The rice and the soup of collected vegetables were cooked with water from the stream that trickled around us, filtered by the water system that the Karen Hilltribes Trust had helped to install. The Karen had also bought some salted fish, which they pounded with grilled chillies to make a rustic, very hot but truly delicious relish, eaten with yet more vegetables. As a cook, it was a magical experience to see these people, collecting and then cooking their food so quickly.

"I was so delighted by the picnic that I offered money to the guys who had made the day so memorable. Embarrassed Salahae frowned and shook his head. He was uncomfortable refusing me, but explained he did not want anyone to associate money with the generosity and hospitality their culture obliges them to offer. I was just left admiring his wisdom – and the spirit of the Karen. Perhaps next time, I'll take a larger bottle of Campari – and an extra tot of gin for Grandma and me."

Other Sources of Reference

The Karen People of Burma – Harry Ignatius Marshall

Peoples of the Golden Triangle – Paul & Elaine Lewis

Forest Guardians, Forest Destroyers The Politics of Environmental Knowledge in Northern Thailand – Tim Forsyth & Andrew Walker

For more information about the Karen Hilltribes Trust please contact:

Penelope Worsley, Karen Hilltribes Trust, 88a Main Street, Fulford, York, YO10 5DX
email: penelopeworsley@gmail.com
or visit the website: www.karenhilltribes.org.uk.

For more information about Huntington's Disease please contact:

The Huntington's Disease Association
Neurosupport Centre, Norton Street, Liverpool, L3 8LR
Tel: 0151 298 3298
email: info@hda.org.uk
or visit the website: www.hda.org.uk